Silencing the Past

Beacon Press Boston

Silencing the Past

Power and
the Production
of History

Michel-Rolph Trouillot

Beacon Press
25 Beacon Street
Boston, Massachusetts 02108-2892

Beacon Press books
are published under the auspices of
the Unitarian Universalist Association of Congregations.

Printed in the United States of America

Illustrations: Henry I, King of Haiti, courtesy Institut de Sauvegarde du Patrimoine National (ISPAN); Sans Souci–Milot, today, courtesy ISPAN; Sans Souci–Milot, a nineteenth-century engraving, courtesy ISPAN; Battle in Saint-Domingue, courtesy Fondation pour la Recherche Iconographique et Documentaire; Columbus's landing, courtesy Afriques en Création.

05 10 9

Text design by Susan Hochbaum
Composition by Wilsted & Taylor

Library of Congress Cataloging-in-Publication Data
Trouillot, Michel-Rolph.
Silencing the past : power and the production of history / Michel-Rolph Trouillot.
p. cm.
Includes bibliographical references and index.
ISBN 0-8070-4310-9 (cloth)
ISBN 0-8070-4311-7 (paper)
1. Historicism. 2. Power (Philosophy). 3. Historiography. I. Title.
D16.9.T85 1995
901—dc20 95-17665
CIP

To the memory of my father,

Ernst Trouillot

To my mother,

Anne-Marie Morisset

I am well aware
that by no means
equal repute
attends the narrator
and the doer of deeds.

Sallust
History of Catiline

Contents

Acknowledgments

I have carried this book in so many shapes and to so many places that in no way can I measure the debts accumulated along the way. My trail of paper and diskettes cannot adequately register why a particular scene became a *relievo* or when a particular argument became mine.

Time is not the only reason I cannot retrace all my debts: this book stands at the junction of emotive and intellectual communities that it straddles and unites without closure. Ernst and Hénock Trouillot influenced this project both during their lifetime and from beyond the grave in ways that are both transparent and intricate. I cannot date my interest in the production of history, but my first conscious marker is my perusal of the work they coauthored with Catts Pressoir, the first historiography book I read. They and other Haitian writers who preceded them are still privileged interlocutors at the boundaries of a custom-made intellectual community of relatives and friends I have in mind whatever I write. At the living center of that intellectual community, Michel Acacia, Pierre Buteau, Jean Coulanges, Lyonel Trouillot, Evelyne Trouillot-Ménard, and Drexel Woodson—who is too close to me and to Haiti not to be drafted into the family—have provided inspiration, comments, tips, and criticisms. I know that words are not enough, but *mèsi anpil.*

I started to write on the production of history as a distinct topic in 1981. Some of these writings found a transcontinental community of debate in 1985 when David W. Cohen asked me to join the International Roundtable in History and Anthropology. My involvement in the Roundtables, my continuous and fruitful exchanges with other participants, including David himself, influenced my grasp of some of the issues treated here. Both chapters 1 and 2 evolved in different ways from papers I originally prepared for the Fifth and Sixth International Roundtables, respectively held in Paris in 1986 and Bellagio in 1989.

Johns Hopkins University constitutes a third intellectual community that made this book possible. For the last six years, the Homewood campus provided my most demanding grounds for testing specific ideas: graduate and faculty seminars, and the most difficult audience to convince—students. Recurrent conversations in my theory classes, in the seminar on "The Perspective of the World," in the seminar in methodology in anthropology and history I taught with Sara Berry, and the general seminar of the Institute for Global Studies in Culture, Power and History helped me find the proper expression for many of the ideas exposed here. My colleague Sara S. Berry has been a generous intellectual companion, a stimulating source of ideas, and a sharp critic. Her formulations helped me to articulate some of my views. My colleagues in the Department of Anthropology during the years this book matured have been supportive friends and daily interlocutors: Eytan Bercovitch, Gillian Feeley-Harnik, Ashraf Ghani, Niloofar Haeri, Emily Martin, Sidney W. Mintz, Katherine Verdery, and, more recently, Yun-Xiang Yan. Sid's vast knowledge greatly improved chapter 4. Niloofar coached me on language matters, such as evidentials. Katherine commented on multiple versions of various chapters. Brackette F. Williams moved in as I was nearly finished but early enough to make the usual difference, especially in chapter 5. For the third time we were neighbors; for the third time, the intellectual landscape changed.

I owe more to my students than they will ever know, the undergraduates from different classes and, especially, the Ph.D. candidates in anthropology and history who worked with me on issues that touched the production of history. Pamela Ballinger, April Hartfield, Fred Klaits, Kira Kosnick, Christopher McIntyre, Viranjini Munasinghe, Eric P. Rice, Hanan Sabea, and Nathalie Zacek are among those whose reactions to my ideas and specific comments on parts of this book forced me to revisit points I thought obvious.

Previous versions of parts of this book were published in *Public Culture* and the *Journal of Caribbean History.* I thank both publications for the opportunity of publishing these earlier articles and for the permission to reprint here. I also presented parts of this book in a number of academic settings: the International Roundtables in History and Anthropology, the conference "Révolution Haïtienne et Révolution Française" (Port-au-Prince, Haiti, 12 December 1989), and various seminars at Harvard, the University of Michigan, the University of Pennsylvania, and Johns Hopkins University. In each case, I benefited from stimulating discussions. David W. Cohen, Joan DeJean, Nancy Farriss, Dorothy Ross, Doris Sommer, Rebecca Scott, and William Rowe deserve special thanks for making these encounters both possible and fruitful. I also thank the institutions mentioned, as well as the Maison des Sciences de l'Homme, Paris, and the Max Plank Institut, Göttingen, which cosponsored the Roundtables.

A number of institutions provided support for the research, writing, and editing that went into this book: the National Humanities Center, the John Simon Guggenheim Foundation, the

Woodrow Wilson International Center for Scholars, and Johns Hopkins University. Special thanks to Charles Blitzer who was twice a gracious host.

A number of individuals worked closely with me on the final version. Elizabeth Dunn provided research assistance on memory and commented on chapter 1. Anne-Carine Trouillot's comments were useful throughout and her help was crucial to chapter 4. Rebecca Bennette, Nadève Ménard, and Hilbert Shin commented on various parts of the final draft and assisted me both in research and throughout the final writing and editing. I thank them for having not rebelled more often. Special thanks to Hilbert Shin for protecting my research time. Deb Chasman, my editor at Beacon Press, nurtured this book with care and attention. Her extraordinary patience, her contagious enthusiasm, and her close collaboration made its completion possible. To Wendy Strothman, Ken Wong, Tisha Hooks, and the rest of the Beacon team, thanks also for sharing that enthusiasm. Warm thanks to Marlowe Bergendoff for her sensitive copy editing.

Both within and beyond the boundaries of these overlapping communities of labor, interest, and emotion, a number of individuals stand out for different reasons. From a vague suggestion that turned into a great lead, from a carefully written comment to a newspaper clip, or a document they took the pains to unearth especially for me, they have made subtle yet significant differences in the outcome. Some of them I have not yet named. Others will suffer an additional mention. Arjun Appadurai, Pamela Ballinger, Sara Berry, Carol A. Breckenridge, Pierre Buteau, David W. Cohen, Joan Dayan, Patrick Delatour, Daniel Elie, Nancy Farriss, Fred Klaits, Peter Hulme, Richard Kagan, Albert Mangones, Hans Medick, Sidney W. Mintz, Viranjini Munasinghe, Michèle Oriol, J. G. A. Pocock, Eric P. Rice, Hanan Sabea, Louis Sala-Molins, Gerald Sider, Gavin Smith, John Thornton, Anne-Carine Trouillot, Lyonel Trouillot, Katherine Verdery, Ronald

Walters, and Drexel Woodson contributed to this book in various ways. Understandably, their input—and that of others—led to results they did not always intend.

I started these acknowledgments with family. I will also end there. My uncle, Lucien Morisset, provided a much-needed and idyllic retreat in Saint-Paul de Vence, where chapter 1 took definitive form and where the book finally emerged as a single whole. Anne-Carine and Canel Trouillot provided both the context of work and the context away from work. They added meaning to this and other ventures. I thank them for their presence and for mediating on the home front the pain and the perverse pleasure of writing in a second language.

Preface

I grew up in a family where history sat at the dinner table. All his life, my father engaged in a number of parallel professional activities, none of which alone defined him, but most of which were steeped in his love of history. I was in my teens when he started a regular program on Haitian television that explored little-known details of the history of the country. That program rarely surprised me: the stories my dad told his audience were not different from those he told at home. I had catalogued some of them on the yellowed cards that embodied a massive biographical dictionary of Haitian history my father never finished. Later, in the class he taught in world history in my high school, I worked harder than my classmates to earn a passing grade. But his lectures, good as they were, never matched what I learned at home on Sundays.

Sunday afternoon was when my father's brother, my uncle Hénock, came to visit. He was one of the few people I knew who actually earned a living from knowing history. He was nominally the director of the National Archives, but writing was his true passion and he published historical research too fast for most readers to keep up with—in books, journals, and newspapers, at times his preferred medium. On Sundays, he tested his ideas on my dad, for whom history was increasingly becoming only a favorite hobby as his law practice expanded. The brothers disagreed more often than not, in part because they genuinely saw the world quite differently, in part because the heat of their divergences, both political and philosophical, fueled their ceremonial of love.

Sunday afternoon was ritual time for the Trouillot brothers. History was their alibi for expressing both their love and their disagreements—with Hénock overplaying his bohemian side and my father stressing bourgeois rationality. They argued about long-dead figures, Haitian and foreign, the way one chats about neighbors—with the concerned distance that comes from knowing intimate details of the lives of people who are not family.

Were I not suspicious of obvious genealogies, I could claim this mixture of intimacy and distance, and the class, race, and gender positions that made it possible, as the central part of my intellectual heritage. But I have learned on my own that the point about such claims may be less what they assert than the fact of their assertion. Growing up who I was, I could not escape historicity, but I also learned that anyone anywhere with the right dosage of suspicion can formulate questions to history with no pretense that these questions themselves stand outside history.

Long before I read Nietzsche's *Untimely Meditations*, I knew intuitively that people can suffer from historical overdose, complaisant hostages of the pasts they create. We learned that much in many Haitian households at the peak of the Duvaliers' terror, if only we dared to look outside. Yet being who I am and looking at the world from there, the mere proposition that one could—or should—escape history seems to me either foolish or deceitful. I find it hard to harness respect for those who genuinely believe that postmodernity, whatever it may be, allows us to claim no roots. I wonder why they have convictions, if indeed they have any. Similarly, allegations that we have reached the end of history or that we are somewhat closer to a future when all pasts will be equal make me wonder about the motives of those who make such claims. I am aware that there is an inherent tension in suggesting that we should acknowledge our position while taking distance from it, but I find that tension both healthy and pleasant. I guess that, after all, I am perhaps claiming that legacy of intimacy and estrangement.

We are never as steeped in history as when we pretend not to be, but if we stop pretending we may gain in understanding what we lose in false innocence. Naiveté is often an excuse for those who exercise power. For those upon whom that power is exercised, naiveté is always a mistake.

This book is about history and power. It deals with the many ways in which the production of historical narratives involves the uneven contribution of competing groups and individuals who have unequal access to the means for such production. The forces I will expose are less visible than gunfire, class property, or political crusades. I want to argue that they are no less powerful.

I also want to reject both the naive proposition that we are prisoners of our pasts and the pernicious suggestion that history is whatever we make of it. History is the fruit of power, but power itself is never so transparent that its analysis becomes superfluous. The ultimate mark of power may be its invisibility; the ultimate challenge, the exposition of its roots.

Silencing the Past

The Power in the Story

 1

This is a story within a story—so slippery at the edges that one wonders when and where it started and whether it will ever end. By the middle of February 1836, the army of general Antonio López de Santa Anna had reached the crumbling walls of the old mission of San Antonio de Valero in the Mexican province of Tejas. Few traces of the Franciscan priests who had built the mission more than a century before had survived the combined assaults of time and of a succession of less religious residents. Intermittent squatters, Spanish and Mexican soldiers, had turned the place into something of a fort and nicknamed it "the Alamo," from the name of a Spanish cavalry unit that undertook one of the many transformations of the crude compound. Now, three years after Santa Anna first gained power in independent Mexico, a few English-speaking squatters occupied the place, refusing to surrender to his superior force. Luckily for Santa Anna, the squatters were outnumbered—at most 189 potential fighters—and the structure itself was weak. The conquest would be easy, or so thought Santa Anna.

The conquest was not easy: the siege persisted through twelve days of cannonade. On March 6, Santa Anna blew the horns that Mexicans traditionally used to announce an attack to the death.

Later on that same day, his forces finally broke through the fort, killing most of the defenders. But a few weeks later, on April 21, at San Jacinto, Santa Anna fell prisoner to Sam Houston, the freshly certified leader of the secessionist Republic of Texas.

Santa Anna recovered from that upset; he went on to be four more times the leader of a much reduced Mexico. But in important ways, he was doubly defeated at San Jacinto. He lost the battle of the day, but he also lost the battle he had won at the Alamo. Houston's men had punctuated their victorious attack on the Mexican army with repeated shouts of "Remember the Alamo! Remember the Alamo!" With that reference to the old mission, they doubly made history. As actors, they captured Santa Anna and neutralized his forces. As narrators, they gave the Alamo story a new meaning. The military loss of March was no longer the end point of the narrative but a necessary turn in the plot, the trial of the heroes, which, in turn, made final victory both inevitable and grandiose. With the battle cry of San Jacinto, Houston's men reversed for more than a century the victory Santa Anna thought he had gained in San Antonio.

Human beings participate in history both as actors and as narrators. The inherent ambivalence of the word "history" in many modern languages, including English, suggests this dual participation. In vernacular use, history means both the facts of the matter and a narrative of those facts, both "what happened" and "that which is said to have happened." The first meaning places the emphasis on the sociohistorical process, the second on our knowledge of that process or on a story about that process.

If I write "The history of the United States begins with the Mayflower," a statement many readers may find simplistic and controversial, there will be little doubt that I am suggesting that the first significant event in the process that eventuated in what we now call the United States is the landing of the Mayflower. Consider now a sentence grammatically identical to the preceding one and perhaps as controversial: "The history of France starts with Michelet." The meaning of the word "history" has unambiguously shifted from the sociohistorical process to our knowledge of that process. The sentence affirms that the first significant narrative about France was the one written by Jules Michelet.

Yet the distinction between what happened and that which is said to have happened is not always clear. Consider a third sentence: "The history of the United States is a history of migration." The reader may choose to understand both uses of the word history as emphasizing the sociohistorical process. Then, the sentence seems to suggest that the fact of migration is the central element in the evolution of the United States. But an equally valid interpretation of that sentence is that the best narrative about the United States is a story of migrations. That interpretation becomes privileged if I add a few qualifiers: "The true history of the United States is a history of migrations. That history remains to be written."

Yet a third interpretation may place the emphasis on the sociohistorical process for the first use of the word "history" and on knowledge and narrative for its second use in the same sentence, thus suggesting that the best narrative about the United States is one of which migration is the central theme. This third interpretation is possible only because we implicitly acknowledge an overlap between the sociohistorical process and our knowledge of it, an overlap significant enough to allow us to suggest, with varying degree of metaphorical intent, that the history of the United States is a story of migrations. Not only can history mean either the sociohistorical process or our knowledge of that process, but the boundary between the two meanings is often quite fluid.

The vernacular use of the word history thus offers us a semantic ambiguity: an irreducible distinction and yet an equally irreducible overlap between what happened and that which is said to have happened. Yet it suggests also the importance of context: the overlap and the distance between the two sides of historicity may not be susceptible to a general formula. The ways in which what happened and that which is said to have happened are and are not the same may itself be historical.

Words are not concepts and concepts are not words: between the two are the layers of theory accumulated throughout the ages. But theories are built on words and with words. Thus it is not surprising that the ambiguity offered by the vernacular use of the word history has caught the attention of many thinkers since at least antiquity. What is surprising is the reluctance with which theories of history have dealt with this fundamental ambiguity. Indeed, as history became a distinguishable profession, theorists have followed two incompatible tendencies. Some, influenced by positivism, have emphasized the distinction between the historical world and what we say or write about it. Others, who adopt a "constructivist" viewpoint, have stressed the overlap between the historical process and narratives about that process. Most have treated the combination itself, the core of the ambiguity, as if it were a mere accident of vernacular parlance to be corrected by theory. What I hope to do is to show how much room there is to look at the production of history outside of the dichotomies that these positions suggest and reproduce.

One-sided Historicity

Summaries of intellectual trends and subdisciplines always shortchange the various authors they somewhat compulsively regroup. I do not even attempt such a regrouping here. I hope that the following sketch is sufficient to show the limitations that I question.[1]

Positivism has a bad name today, but at least some of that scorn is well deserved. As history solidified as a profession in the nineteenth century, scholars significantly influenced by positivist views tried to theorize the distinction between historical process and historical knowledge. Indeed, the professionalization of the discipline is partly premised on that distinction: the more distant the sociohistorical process is from its knowledge, the easier the claim to a "scientific" professionalism. Thus, historians and, more particularly, philosophers of history were proud to discover or reiterate instances where the distinction was supposedly indisputable because it was marked not only by semantic context, but by morphology or by the lexicon itself. The Latin distinction between *res gesta* and *(historia) rerum gestarum*, or the German distinction between *Geschichte* and *Geschichtschreibung*, helped to inscribe a fundamental difference, sometimes ontological, sometimes epistemological, between what happened and what was said to have happened. These philosophical boundaries, in turn, reinforced the chronological boundary between past and present inherited from antiquity.

The positivist position dominated Western scholarship enough to influence the vision of history among historians and philosophers who did not necessarily see themselves as positivists. Tenets of that vision still inform the public's sense of history in most of Europe and North America: the role of the historian is to reveal the past, to discover or, at least, approximate the truth. Within that viewpoint, power is unproblematic, irrelevant to the construction of the narrative as such. At best, history is a story about power, a story about those who won.

The proposition that history is another form of fiction is almost as old as history itself, and the arguments used to defend it have varied greatly. As Tzvetan Todorov suggests, there is nothing new even in the claim that everything is an interpretation, except the euphoria that now surrounds the claim.[2] What I call the constructivist view of history is a particular version of these two propositions that has gained visibility in academe since the 1970s. It builds upon recent advances in critical theory, in the theory of the narrative and analytic philosophy. In its dominant version, it contends that the historical narrative bypasses the issue of truth by virtue of its form. Narratives are necessarily emplotted in a way that life is not. Thus they necessarily distort life whether or not the evidence upon which they are based could be proved correct. Within that viewpoint, history becomes one among many types of narratives with no particular distinction except for its pretense of truth.[3] Whereas the positivist view hides the tropes of power behind a naive epistemology, the constructivist one denies the autonomy of the sociohistorical process. Taken to its logical end point, constructivism views the historical narrative as one fiction among others.

But what makes some narratives rather than others powerful enough to pass as accepted history if not historicity itself? If history is merely the story told by those who won, how did they win in the first place? And why don't all winners tell the same story?

Between Truth and Fiction

Each historical narrative renews a claim to truth.[4] If I write a story describing how U.S. troops entering a German prison at the end of World War II massacred five hundred Gypsies; if I claim this story is based on documents recently found in Soviet archives and corroborated by German sources, and if I fabricate such sources and publish my story as such, I have not written fiction, I have produced a fake. I have violated the rules that govern claims to historical truth.[5] That such rules are not the same in all times and all places has led many scholars to suggest that some societies (non-Western, of course) do not differentiate between fiction and history. That assertion reminds us of past debates among some Western observers about the languages of the peoples they colonized. Because these observers did not find grammar books or dictionaries among the so-called savages, because they could not understand or apply the grammatical rules that governed these languages, they promptly concluded that such rules did not exist.

As befits comparisons between the West and the many subaltern others it created for itself, the field was uneven from the start; the objects contrasted were eminently incomparable. The comparison unfairly juxtaposed a discourse about language and linguistic practice: the metalanguage of grammarians proved the existence of grammar in European languages; spontaneous speech proved its absence elsewhere. Some Europeans and their colonized students saw in this alleged absence of rules the infantile freedom that they came to associate with savagery, while others saw in it one more proof of the inferiority of non-whites. We now know that both sides were wrong; grammar functions in all languages. Could the same be said about history, or is history so infinitely malleable in some societies that it loses its differential claim to truth?

The classification of all non-Westerners as fundamentally non-historical is tied also to the assumption that history requires a linear and cumulative sense of time that allows the observer to isolate the past as a distinct entity. Yet Ibn Khaldhún fruitfully applied a cyclical view of time to the study of history. Further, the exclusive adherence to linear time by Western historians themselves, and the ensuing rejection of the people left "without history" both date from the nineteenth century.[6] Did the West have a history before 1800?

The pernicious belief that epistemic validity matters only to Western-educated populations, either because others lack the proper sense of time or the proper sense of evidence, is belied by the use of *evidentials* in a number of non-European languages.[7] An English approximation would be a rule forcing historians to distinguish grammatically between "I heard that it happened," "I saw it happen," or "I have obtained evidence that it happened" every time they use the verb "to happen." English, of course, has no such grammatical rule for assessing evidence. Does the fact that Tucuya has an elaborate system of evidentials predispose its Amazonian speakers to be better historians than most Englishmen?

Arjun Appadurai argues convincingly that rules about what he calls "the debatability of the past" operate in all societies.[8] Although these rules exhibit substantive variations in time and space, they all aim to guarantee a minimal credibility in history. Appadurai suggests a number of formal constraints that universally enforce that credibility and limit the character of historical debates: authority, continuity, depth, and interdependence. Nowhere is history infinitely susceptible to invention.

The need for a different kind of credibility sets the historical narrative apart from fiction. This need is both contingent and necessary. It is contingent inasmuch as some narratives go back and forth over the line between fiction and history, while others occupy an undefined position that seems to deny the very existence of a line. It is necessary inasmuch as, at some point, historically specific groups of humans must decide if a particular narrative belongs to history or to fiction. In other words, the epistemological break between history and fiction is always expressed concretely through the historically situated evaluation of specific narratives.

Is island cannibalism fact or fiction? Scholars have long tried to confirm or discredit some early Spanish colonizers' contention that Native Americans of the Antilles committed cannibalism.[9] Is the semantic association between Caribs, Cannibals, and Caliban based on more than European phantasms? Some scholars claim that the fantasy has reached such significance for the West that it matters little whether it is based on facts. Does this mean that the line between history and fiction is useless? As long as the conversation involves Europeans talking about dead Indians, the debate is merely academic.

Yet even dead Indians can return to haunt professional and amateur historians. The Inter-Tribal council of American Indians affirms that the remains of more than a thousand individuals, mostly Native American Catholics, are buried in grounds adjacent to the Alamo, in an old cemetery once linked to the Franciscan mission, but of which the most visible traces have disappeared. The council's efforts to have the sacredness of the grounds recognized by the state of Texas and the city of San Antonio have met only partial success. Still, they are impressive enough to threaten the control the organization that has custody of the Alamo, the Daughters of the Republic of Texas, holds over a historical site entrusted to them by the state since 1905.

The debate over the grounds fits within a larger war that some observers have dubbed "the second battle of the Alamo." That larger controversy surrounds the 1836 siege of the compound by Santa Anna's forces. Is that battle a moment of glory during which freedom-loving Anglos, outnumbered but undaunted, spontaneously chose to fight until death rather than surrender to a corrupt Mexican dictator? Or is it a brutal example of U.S. expansionism, the story of a few white predators taking over what was sacred territory and half-willingly providing, with their death, the alibi for a well-planned annexation? So phrased the debate evokes issues that have divided a few historians and inhabitants of Texas over the last twenty years. But with San Antonio's population now composed of 56 percent nominal Hispanics, many of whom also acknowledge some Native American ancestry, "the second battle of the Alamo" has literally reached the streets. Demonstrations, parades, editorials, and demands for various municipal or court orders—including one blocking the streets now leading to the Alamo—punctuate the debate between increasingly angry parties.

In the heated context of this debate, advocates on both sides are questioning factual statements, the accuracy of which mattered to few half a century ago. "Facts," both trivial or prominent in relative isolation, are questioned or heralded by each camp.

. . . .

Historians had long questioned the veracity of some of the events in Alamo narratives, most notably the story of the line on the ground. According to that story, when it became clear that the choice for the 189 Alamo occupants was between escape and certain death at the Mexicans' hands, commandant William Barret Travis drew a line on the ground. He then asked all those willing to fight to the death to cross it. Supposedly, everyone crossed—except of course the man who conveniently escaped to tell the story. Texas historians, and especially Texas-based authors of textbooks and popular history, long concurred that this particular narrative was only "a good story," and that "it doesn't really matter whether it is true or not."[10] Such remarks were made before the current constructivist wave by people who otherwise believed that facts are facts and nothing but facts. But in a context where the courage of the men who stayed at the Alamo is openly questioned, the line on the ground is suddenly among the many "facts" now submitted to a test of credibility.

The list is endless.[11] Where exactly was the cemetery, and are the remains still there? Are tourist visits to the Alamo violating the religious rights of the dead and should the state of Texas intervene? Did the state itself ever pay the Roman Catholic Church the agreed-upon price for the chapel of the Alamo and, if not, are not the custodians usurpers of a historical landmark? Did James

Bowie, one of the white American leaders, bury a stolen treasure in the site? If so, is that the real reason why the occupants chose to fight or, conversely, did Bowie try to negotiate in order to save both his life and the treasure? In short, how much was greed, rather than patriotism, central to the Alamo battle? Did the besieged mistakenly believe that reinforcement was on its way and, if so, how much can we believe in their courage? Did Davy Crockett die during the battle or after the battle? Did he try to surrender? Did he really wear a coonskin cap?

That last question may sound the most trivial of a rather bizarre list; but it appears less trifling and not at all bizarre when we note that the Alamo shrine is Texas's main tourist attraction, drawing some three million visitors a year. Now that local voices have become loud enough to question the innocence of a little *gringo* wearing a Davy cap, mom and dad may think twice about buying one, and the custodians of history shiver, afraid that the past is catching up too fast with the present. In the context of that controversy, it suddenly matters how real Davy was.

The lesson of the debate is clear. At some stage, for reasons that are themselves historical, most often spurred by controversy, collectivities experience the need to impose a test of credibility on certain events and narratives because it matters *to them* whether these events are true or false, whether these stories are fact or fiction.

That it matters to them does not necessarily mean that it matters to us. But how far can we carry our isolationism? Does it really not matter whether or not the dominant narrative of the Jewish Holocaust is true or false? Does it really not make a difference whether or not the leaders of Nazi Germany actually planned and supervised the death of six million Jews?

The associates of the Institute for Historical Review maintain that the Holocaust narrative matters, but they also maintain that it is false. They generally agree that Jews were victimized during

World War II, and some even accept that the Holocaust was a tragedy. However, most profess to set the record straight on three main issues: the reported number of six million Jews killed by the Nazis; the systematic Nazi plan for the extermination of Jews; the existence of "gas chambers" for mass murders.[12] Revisionists claim there is no irrefutable evidence to back any of these central "facts" of the dominant Holocaust narrative which serves only to perpetuate various state policies in the United States, Europe, and Israel.

Revisionist theses on the Holocaust have been refuted by a number of authors. Historian Pierre Vidal-Naquet, whose own mother died at Auschwitz, has used his repeated rebuttals of revisionist theses to raise powerful questions on the relation between scholarship and political responsibility. Jean-Pierre Pressac, himself a former revisionist, documents better than any other historian the German death machinery. Deborah Lipstadt's most recent book on the subject examines the political motivations of the revisionists in order to launch an ideological critique of revisionism. To that latter kind of critique, the revisionists reply that they are historians: why should their motives matter if they follow "the customary methods of historical criticism"? We can't dismiss heliocentric theory just because Copernicus apparently hated the Catholic Church.[13]

The revisionists' claimed adherence to empiricist procedures provides a perfect case to test the limits of historical constructionism.[14] The immediate political and moral stakes of Holocaust narratives for a number of constituencies worldwide, and the competing strength and loudness of these constituencies in the United States and in Europe leave the constructivists both politically and theoretically naked. For the only logical constructivist position on the Holocaust debate is to deny that there is matter to debate. Constructivists must claim that it does not really matter whether or not there were gas chambers, whether the death toll was one or six million, or whether the genocide was planned. And indeed, constructivist Hayden White came dangerously close to suggesting that the main relevance of the dominant Holocaust narrative is that it serves to legitimate the policies of the state of Israel.[15] White later qualified his extreme constructivist stance and now espouses a much more modest relativism.[16]

But how much can we reduce what happened to what is said to have happened? If six million do not really matter, would two million be enough, or would some of us settle for three hundred thousand? If meaning is totally severed from a referent "out there," if there is no cognitive purpose, nothing to be proved or disproved, what then is the point of the story? White's answer is clear: to establish moral authority. But why bother with the Holocaust or plantation slavery, Pol Pot, or the French Revolution, when we already have Little Red Riding Hood?

Constructivism's dilemma is that *while it can point to hundreds of stories that illustrate its general claim that narratives are produced, it cannot give a full account of the production of any single narrative*. For either we would all share the same stories of legitimation, or the reasons why a specific story matters to a specific population are themselves historical. To state that a particular narrative legitimates particular policies is to refer implicitly to a "true" account of these policies through time, an account which itself can take the form of another narrative. But to admit the possibility of this second narrative is, in turn, to admit that the historical process has some autonomy vis-à-vis the narrative. It is to admit that as ambiguous and contingent as it is, the boundary between what happened and that which is said to have happened is necessary.

It is not that some societies distinguish between fiction and history and others do not. Rather, the difference is in the range of narratives that specific collectivities must put to their own tests of historical credibility because of the stakes involved in these narratives.

Single-site Historicity

We would be wrong to think that such stakes proceed naturally from the importance of the original event. The widespread notion of history as reminiscence of important past experiences is misleading. The model itself is well known: history is to a collectivity as remembrance is to an individual, the more or less conscious retrieval of past experiences stored in memory. Its numerous variations aside, we can call it, for short, the storage model of memory-history.

The first problem with the storage model is its age, the antiquated science upon which it rests. The model assumes a view of knowledge as recollection, which goes back to Plato, a view now disputed by philosophers and cognitive scientists. Further, the vision of individual memory on which it draws has been strongly questioned by researchers of various stripes since at least the end of the nineteenth century. Within that vision, memories are discrete representations stored in a cabinet, the contents of which are generally accurate and accessible at will. Recent research has questioned all these assumptions. Remembering is not always a process of summoning representations of what happened. Tying a shoe involves memory, but few of us engage in an explicit recall of images every time we routinely tie our shoes. Whether or not the distinction between implicit and explicit memory involves different memory systems, the fact that such systems are inextricably linked in practice may be one more reason why explicit memories change. At any rate, there is evidence that the contents of our cabinet are neither fixed nor accessible at will.[17]

Further, were such contents complete, they would not form a

history. Consider a monologue describing in sequence all of an individual's recollections. It would sound as a meaningless cacophony even to the narrator. Further, it is at least possible that events otherwise significant to the life trajectory were not known to the individual at the time of occurrence and cannot be told as remembered experiences. The individual can only remember the revelation, not the event itself. I may remember that I went to Japan without remembering what it felt like to be in Japan. I may remember being told that my parents took me to Japan when I was six months old. But then, is it only the revelation that belongs to my life history? Can we confidently exclude from one's history all events not experienced or not yet revealed, including, for instance, an adoption at the time of birth? An adoption might provide a crucial perspective on episodes that actually occurred before its revelation. The revelation itself may affect the narrator's future memory of events that happened *before*.

If memories as individual history are constructed, even in this minimal sense, how can the past they retrieve be fixed? The storage model has no answer to that problem. Both its popular and scholarly versions assume the independent existence of a fixed past and posit memory as the retrieval of that content. But the past does not exist independently from the present. Indeed, the past is only past because there is a present, just as I can point to something *over there* only because I am *here*. But nothing is inherently over there or here. In that sense, the past has no content. The past—or, more accurately, pastness—is a position. Thus, in no way can we identify the past *as past*. Leaving aside for now the fact that my knowledge that I once went to Japan, however derived, may not be of the same nature as remembering what it was like to be in Japan, the model assumes that both kinds of information exist *as past* prior to my retrieval. But how do I retrieve them as past without prior knowledge or memory of what constitutes pastness?

The problems of determining what belongs to the past multiply tenfold when that past is said to be collective. Indeed, when the memory-history equation is transferred to a collectivity, methodological individualism adds its weight to the inherent difficulties of the storage model. We may want to assume for purposes of description that the life history of an individual starts with birth. But when does the life of a collectivity start? At what point do we set the beginning of the past to be retrieved? How do we decide—and how does the collectivity decide—which events to include and which to exclude? The storage model assumes not only the past to be remembered but the collective subject that does the remembering. The problem with this dual assumption is that the constructed past itself is constitutive of the collectivity.

Do Europeans and white Americans remember discovering the New World? Neither Europe as we now know it, nor whiteness as we now experience it, existed as such in 1492. Both are constitutive of this retrospective entity we now call the West, without which the "discovery" is unthinkable in its present form. Can the citizens of Quebec, whose license plates proudly state "I remember," actually retrieve memories of the French colonial state? Can Macedonians, whoever they may be, recall the early conflicts and promises of panhellenism? Can anybody anywhere actually remember the first mass conversions of Serbians to Christianity? In these cases, as in many others, the collective subjects who supposedly remember did not exist as such at the time of the events they claim to remember. Rather, their constitution as subjects goes hand in hand with the continuous creation of the past. As such, they do not succeed such a past: they are its contemporaries.

Even when the historical continuities are unquestionable, in no way can we assume a simple correlation between the magnitude of events as they happened and their relevance for the generations that inherit them through history. The comparative study of slavery in the Americas provides an engaging example that what we often call the "legacy of the past" may not be anything bequeathed by the past itself.

At first glance, it would seem obvious that the historical relevance of slavery in the United States proceeds from the horrors of the past. That past is constantly evoked as the starting point of an ongoing traumatism and as a necessary explanation to current inequalities suffered by blacks. I would be the last to deny that plantation slavery was a traumatic experience that left strong scars throughout the Americas. But the experience of African-Americans outside of the United States challenges the direct correlation between past traumas and historical relevance.

In the context of the hemisphere, the United States imported a relatively small number of enslaved Africans both before and after its independence. During four centuries, the slave trade delivered at least ten million slaves to the New World. Enslaved Africans worked and died in the Caribbean a century before the settlement of Jamestown, Virginia. Brazil, the territory where slavery lasted longest, received the lion's share of the African slaves, nearly four million. The Caribbean region as a whole imported even more slaves than Brazil, spread among the colonies of various European powers. Still, imports were high among individual Caribbean territories, especially the sugar islands. Thus the French Caribbean island of Martinique, a tiny territory less than one-fourth the size of Long Island, imported more slaves than all the U.S. states combined.[18] To be sure, by the early nineteenth century, the United States had more Creole slaves than any other American country, but this number was due to natural increase. Still, both in terms of its duration and in terms of the number of individuals involved, in no way can we say that the magnitude of U.S. slavery outdid that of Brazil or the Caribbean.

Second, slavery was at least as significant to the daily life of Brazilian and Caribbean societies as to U.S. society as a whole. The British and French sugar islands in particular, from seventeenth-century Barbados and Jamaica to eighteenth-century Saint-Domingue and Martinique, were not simply societies that had slaves: they were *slave societies*. Slavery defined their economic, social, and cultural organization: it was their raison d'être. The people who lived there, free or not, lived there because there were slaves. The northern equivalent would be for the whole continental United States to look like the state of Alabama at the peak of its cotton career.

Third, we need not assume that human suffering can be measured to affirm that the slaves' material conditions were no better outside the United States than within its borders. Allegations of paternalism notwithstanding, we know that U.S. masters were no more humane than their Brazilian or Caribbean counterparts. But we know also that the human toll of slavery, both physical and cultural, was intimately tied to the exigencies of production, notably the work regimen. Working conditions generally imposed lower life expectancy, higher death rates, and much lower birth rates among Caribbean and Brazilian slaves than among their U.S. counterparts.[19] From that viewpoint, sugarcane was the slaves' most sadistic tormentor.

In short, there is a mass of evidence big enough to uphold a modest empirical claim: The impact of slavery as what actually happened cannot in any way be said to have been stronger in the United States than in Brazil and the Caribbean. But then, why is both the symbolic relevance of slavery as trauma and the analytical relevance of slavery as sociohistorical explanation so much more prevalent today in the United States than in Brazil or the Caribbean?

Part of the answer may be the way U.S. slavery ended: a Civil War for which more whites seem to blame the slaves than Abraham Lincoln—whose own motives in the enterprise remain otherwise contested. Part of the answer may be the fate of the slaves' descendants, but that itself is not an issue of "the past." The perpetuation of U.S. racism is less a legacy of slavery than a modern phenomenon renewed by generations of white immigrants whose own ancestors were likely engaged in forced labor, at one time or another, in the hinterlands of Europe.

Indeed, not all blacks who witnessed slavery believed that it was a legacy of which they and their children would forever carry the burden.[20] Half a century after Emancipation, slavery was not a major theme among white historians either, albeit for different reasons. U.S. historiography, for reasons perhaps not too different from its Brazilian counterpart, produced its own silences on African-American slavery. Earlier in this century, there were blacks and whites in North America who argued over both the symbolic and analytical relevance of slavery for the present they were living.[21] Such debates suggest that historical relevance does not proceed directly from the original impact of an event, or its mode of inscription, or even the continuity of that inscription.

Debates about the Alamo, the Holocaust, or the significance of U.S. slavery involve not only professional historians but ethnic and religious leaders, political appointees, journalists, and various associations within civil society as well as independent citizens, not all of whom are activists. This variety of narrators is one of many indications that theories of history have a rather limited view of the field of historical production. They grossly underestimate the size, the relevance, and the complexity of the overlapping sites where history is produced, notably outside of academia.[22]

The strength of the historical guild varies from one society to the next. Even in highly complex societies where the weight of the guild is significant, never does the historians' production constitute a closed corpus. Rather, that production interacts not only with the work of other academics, but importantly also with the history produced outside of the universities. Thus, the thematic awareness of history is not activated only by recognized academics. We are all amateur historians with various degrees of awareness about our production. We also learn history from similar amateurs. Universities and university presses are not the only loci of production of the historical narrative. Books sell even better than coonskin caps at the Alamo gift shop, to which half a dozen titles by amateur historians bring more than $400,000 a year. As Marc Ferro argues, history has many hearths and academics are not the sole history teachers in the land.[23]

Most Europeans and North Americans learn their first history lessons through media that have not been subjected to the standards set by peer reviews, university presses, or doctoral committees. Long before average citizens read the historians who set the standards of the day for colleagues and students, they access history through celebrations, site and museum visits, movies, national holidays, and primary school books. To be sure, the views they learn there are, in turn, sustained, modified, or challenged by scholars involved in primary research. As history continues to solidify professionally, as historians become increasingly quick at modifying their targets and refining their tools for investigation, the impact of academic history increases, even if indirectly.

But let us not forget how fragile, how limited, and how recent that apparent hegemony may be. Let us not forget that, quite recently, in many parts of the United States national and world history prolonged a providential narrative with strong religious undertones. The history of the world then started with Creation, for which the date was supposedly well known, and continued with Manifest Destiny, as befits a country privileged by Divine Providence. American social science has yet to discard the belief in U.S. exceptionalism that permeated its birth and its evolution.[24] Likewise, academic professionalism has not yet silenced creationist history, which is still alive in enclaves within the school system.

That school system may not have the last word on any issue, but its limited efficiency cuts both ways. From the mid 1950s to the late 1960s, Americans learned more about the history of colonial America and the American West from movies and television than from scholarly books. Remember the Alamo? That was a history lesson delivered by John Wayne on the screen. Davy Crockett was a television character who became a significant historical figure rather than the obverse.[25] Before and after Hollywood's long commitment to the history of cowboys and pioneers, comic books rather than textbooks, country songs rather than chronological tables filled the gaps left by the westerns. Then as now, American children and quite a few young males elsewhere learned to thematize parts of that history by playing cowboys and Indians.

Finally, the guild understandably reflects the social and political divisions of American society. Yet, by virtue of its professional claims, the guild cannot express political opinions as such—quite contrary, of course, to activists and lobbyists. Thus, ironically, the more important an issue for specific segments of civil society, the more subdued the interpretations of the facts offered by most professional historians. To a majority of the individuals involved in the controversies surrounding the Columbian quincentennial, the "Last Fact" exhibit at the Smithsonian on the *Enola Gay* and Hiroshima, the excavation of slave cemeteries, or the building of the Vietnam Memorial, the statements produced by most historians seemed often bland or irrelevant. In these cases, as in many others, those to whom history mattered most looked for historical interpretations on the fringes of academia when not altogether outside it.

Yet the fact that history is also produced outside of academia has largely been ignored in theories of history. Beyond a broad—and relatively recent—agreement on the situatedness of the professional historian, there is little concrete exploration of activities that occur elsewhere but impact significantly on the object of study. To be sure, such an impact does not lend itself easily to general formulas, a predicament that rebukes most theorists. I have noted that while most theorists acknowledge at the outset that history involves both the social process and narratives about that process, theories of history actually privilege one side as if the other did not matter.

This one-sidedness is possible because theories of history rarely examine in detail the concrete production of specific narratives. Narratives are occasionally evoked as illustrations or, at best, deciphered as texts, but the process of their production rarely constitutes the object of study.[26] Similarly, most scholars would readily admit that historical production occurs in many sites. But the relative weight of these sites varies with context and these variations impose on the theorist the burden of the concrete. Thus, an examination of French palaces as sites of historical production can provide illustrative lessons for an understanding of Hollywood's role in U.S. historical consciousness, but no abstract theory can set, *a priori*, the rules that govern the relative impact of French castles and of U.S. movies on the academic history produced in these two countries.

The heavier the burden of the concrete, the more likely it is to be bypassed by theory. Thus even the best treatments of academic history proceed as if what happened in the other sites was largely inconsequential. Yet is it really inconsequential that the history of America is being written in the same world where few little boys want to be Indians?

Theorizing Ambiguity and Tracking Power

History is always produced in a specific historical context. Historical actors are also narrators, and vice versa.

The affirmation that narratives are always produced in history leads me to propose two choices. First, I contend that a theory of the historical narrative must acknowledge both the distinction and the overlap between process and narrative. Thus, although this book is primarily about history as knowledge and narrative,[27] it fully embraces the ambiguity inherent in the two sides of historicity.

History, as social process, involves peoples in three distinct capacities: 1) as *agents*, or occupants of structural positions; 2) as *actors* in constant interface with a context; and 3) as *subjects*, that is, as voices aware of their vocality. Classical examples of what I call agents are the strata and sets to which people belong, such as class and status, or the roles associated with these. Workers, slaves, mothers are agents.[28] An analysis of slavery can explore the sociocultural, political, economic, and ideological structures that define such positions as slaves and masters.

By actors, I mean the bundle of capacities that are specific in time and space in ways that both their existence and their understanding rest fundamentally on historical particulars. A comparison of African-American slavery in Brazil and the United States that goes beyond a statistical table must deal with the historical particulars that define the situations being compared. Historical narratives address particular situations and, in that sense, they must deal with human beings as actors.[29]

But peoples are also the subjects of history the way workers are subjects of a strike: they define the very terms under which some situations can be described. Consider a strike as a historical event from a strictly narrative viewpoint, that is, without the interventions that we usually put under such labels as interpretation or explanation. There is no way we can describe a strike without making the subjective capacities of the workers a central part of the description.[30] Stating their absence from the workplace is certainly not enough. We need to state that they collectively reached the decision to stay at home on what was supposed to be a regular working day. We need to add that they collectively acted upon that decision. But even such a description, which takes into account the workers' position as actors, is not a competent description of a strike. Indeed, there are a few other contexts in which such a description could account for something else. Workers could have decided: if the snowfall exceeds ten inches tonight, none of us will come to work tomorrow. If we accept scenarios of manipulation or errors of interpretation among the actors, the possibilities become limitless. Thus, beyond dealing with the workers as actors, a competent narrative of a strike needs to claim access to the workers as purposeful subjects aware of their own voices. It needs their voice(s) in the first person or, at least, it needs to paraphrase that first person. The narrative must give us a hint of both the reasons why the workers refuse to work and the objective they think they are pursuing—even if that objective is limited to the voicing of protest. To put it most simply, a strike is a strike only if the workers think that they are striking. Their subjectivity is an integral part of the event and of any satisfactory description of that event.

Workers work much more often than they strike, but the capacity to strike is never fully removed from the condition of workers. In other words, peoples are not always subjects constantly confronting history as some academics would wish, but the capacity upon which they act to become subjects is always part of their condition. This subjective capacity ensures confusion because it makes human beings doubly historical or, more properly, fully historical. It engages them simultaneously in the sociohistorical process and in narrative constructions about that process. The embracing of this ambiguity, which is inherent in what I call the two sides of historicity, is the first choice of this book.

The second choice of this book is a concrete focus on the process of historical production rather than an abstract concern for the nature of history. The search for the nature of history has led us to deny ambiguity and either to demarcate precisely and at all times the dividing line between historical process and historical knowledge or to conflate at all times historical process and historical narrative. Thus between the mechanically "realist" and naively "constructivist" extremes, there is the more serious task of determining not what history is—a hopeless goal if phrased in essentialist terms—but how history works. For what history is changes with time and place or, better said, history reveals itself only through the production of specific narratives. What matters most are the process and conditions of production of such narratives. Only a focus on that process can uncover the ways in which the two sides of historicity intertwine in a particular context. Only through that overlap can we discover the differential exercise of power that makes some narratives possible and silences others.

Tracking power requires a richer view of historical production than most theorists acknowledge. We cannot exclude in advance any of the actors who participate in the production of history or any of the sites where that production may occur. Next to professional historians we discover artisans of different kinds, unpaid or unrecognized field laborers who augment, deflect, or reorganize the work of the professionals as politicians, students, fiction writers, filmmakers, and participating members of the public. In so doing, we gain a more complex view of academic history itself, since we do not consider professional historians the sole participants in its production.

This more comprehensive view expands the chronological boundaries of the production process. We can see that process as both starting earlier and going on later than most theorists admit. The process does not stop with the last sentence of a professional historian since the public is quite likely to contribute to history if only by adding its own readings to—and about—the scholarly productions. More important, perhaps, since the overlap between history as social process and history as knowledge is fluid, participants in any event may enter into the production of a narrative about that event before the historian as such reaches the scene. In fact, the historical narrative within which an actual event fits could precede that event itself, at least in theory, but perhaps also in practice. Marshall Sahlins suggests that the Hawaiians read their encounter with Captain Cook as the chronicle of a death foretold. But such exercises are not limited to the peoples without historians. How much do narratives of the end of the cold war fit into a prepackaged history of capitalism in knightly armor? William Lewis suggests that one of Ronald Reagan's political strengths was his capacity to inscribe his presidency into a prepackaged narrative about the United States. And an overall sketch of world historical production through time suggests that professional historians alone do not set the narrative framework into which their stories fit. Most often, someone else has already entered the scene and set the cycle of silences.[31]

Does this expanded view still allow pertinent generalizations about the production of the historical narrative? The answer to this question is an unqualified yes, if we agree that such generalizations enhance our understanding of specific practices but do not provide blueprints that practice will supposedly follow or illustrate.

Silences enter the process of historical production at four crucial moments: the moment of fact creation (the making of *sources*); the moment of fact assembly (the making of *archives*); the moment of fact retrieval (the making of *narratives*); and the moment of retrospective significance (the making of *history* in the final instance).

These moments are conceptual tools, second-level abstractions of processes that feed on each other. As such, they are not meant to provide a realistic description of the making of any individual narrative. Rather, they help us understand why not all silences are equal and why they cannot be addressed—or redressed—in the same manner. To put it differently, any historical narrative is a particular bundle of silences, the result of a unique process, and the operation required to deconstruct these silences will vary accordingly.

The strategies deployed in this book reflect these variations. Each of the narratives treated in the next three chapters combines diverse types of silences. In each case, these silences crisscross or accumulate over time to produce a unique mixture. In each case I use a different approach to reveal the conventions and the tensions within that mixture.

In chapter 2, I sketch the image of a former slave turned colonel, now a forgotten figure of the Haitian Revolution. The evidence required to tell his story was available in the corpus I studied, in spite of the poverty of the sources. I only reposition that evidence to generate a new narrative. My alternative narrative, as it develops, reveals the silences that buried, until now, the story of the colonel.

The general silencing of the Haitian Revolution by Western historiography is the subject of chapter 3. That silencing also is due to uneven power in the production of sources, archives, and narratives. But if I am correct that this revolution was unthinkable as it happened, the insignificance of the story is already inscribed in the sources, regardless of what else they reveal. There are no new facts here; not even neglected ones. Here, I have to make the silences speak for themselves. I do so by juxtaposing the climate of the times, the writings of historians on the revolution itself, and narratives of world history where the effectiveness of the original silence becomes fully visible.

The discovery of America, the theme of chapter 4, provided me with yet another combination, thus compelling yet a third strategy. Here was an abundance of both sources and narratives. Until

1992, there was even a sense—although forged and recent—of global agreement on the significance of Columbus's first trip. The main tenets of historical writings were inflected and bolstered through public celebrations that seemed to reinforce this significance. Within this wide-open corpus, silences are produced not so much by an absence of facts or interpretations as through conflicting appropriations of Columbus's persona. Here, I do not suggest a new reading of the same story, as I do in chapter 2, or even alternative interpretations, as in chapter 3. Rather, I show how the alleged agreement about Columbus actually masks a history of conflicts. The methodological exercise culminates in a narrative about the competing appropriations of the discovery. Silences appear in the interstices of the conflicts between previous interpreters.

The production of a historical narrative cannot be studied, therefore, through a mere chronology of its silences. The moments I distinguish here overlap in real time. As heuristic devices, they only crystallize aspects of historical production that best expose when and where power gets into the story.

But even this phrasing is misleading if it suggests that power exists outside the story and can therefore be blocked or excised. Power is constitutive of the story. Tracking power through various "moments" simply helps emphasize the fundamentally processual character of historical production, to insist that what history is matters less than how history works; that power itself works together with history; and that the historians' claimed political preferences have little influence on most of the actual practices of power. A warning from Foucault is helpful: "I don't believe that the question of 'who exercises power?' can be resolved unless that other question '*how does it happen?*' is resolved at the same time."[32]

Power does not enter the story once and for all, but at different times and from different angles. It precedes the narrative proper, contributes to its creation and to its interpretation. Thus, it remains pertinent even if we can imagine a totally scientific history, even if we relegate the historians' preferences and stakes to a separate, post-descriptive phase. In history, power begins at the source.

The play of power in the production of alternative narratives begins with the joint creation of facts and sources for at least two reasons. First, facts are never meaningless: indeed, they become facts only because they matter in some sense, however minimal. Second, facts are not created equal: the production of traces is always also the creation of silences. Some occurrences are noted from the start; others are not. Some are engraved in individual or collective bodies; others are not. Some leave physical markers; others do not. What happened leaves traces, some of which are quite concrete—buildings, dead bodies, censuses, monuments, diaries, political boundaries—that limit the range and significance of any historical narrative. This is one of many reasons why not any fiction can pass for history: the materiality of the socio-historical process (historicity 1) sets the stage for future historical narratives (historicity 2).

The materiality of this first moment is so obvious that some of us take it for granted. It does not imply that facts are meaningless objects waiting to be discovered under some timeless seal but rather, more modestly, that history begins with bodies and artifacts: living brains, fossils, texts, buildings.[33]

The bigger the material mass, the more easily it entraps us: mass graves and pyramids bring history closer while they make us feel small. A castle, a fort, a battlefield, a church, all these things bigger than we that we infuse with the reality of past lives, seem to speak of an immensity of which we know little except that we are part of it. Too solid to be unmarked, too conspicuous to be candid, they embody the ambiguities of history. They give us the power to touch it, but not that to hold it firmly in our hands—hence the mystery of their battered walls. We suspect that their concreteness hides secrets so deep that no revelation may fully dissipate their silences. We imagine the lives under the mortar, but how do we recognize the end of a bottomless silence?

The Three Faces of Sans Souci

Glory and Silences in the Haitian Revolution

 2

I walked in silence between the old walls, trying to guess at the stories they would never dare tell. I had been in the fort since daybreak. I had lost my companions on purpose: I wanted to tiptoe alone through the remains of history. Here and there, I touched a stone, a piece of iron hanging from the mortar, overlooked or left by unknown hands for unknown reasons. I almost tripped over a rail track, a deep cut on the concrete floor, which led to a piece of artillery lost in a darkened corner.

At the end of the alley, the sunlight caught me by surprise. I saw the grave at once, an indifferent piece of cement lying in the middle of the open courtyard. Crossing the Place d'Armes, I imagined the royal cavalry, black-skinned men and women one and all on their black horses, swearing to fight until the death rather than to let go of this fort and return to slavery.

I stepped across my dreams up to the pile of concrete. As I moved closer, the letters on the stone became more visible. I did not need to read the inscription to know the man who was lying under the concrete. This was his fort, his kingdom, the most daring of his buildings—The Citadel, his legacy of stone and arrogance. I bent over, letting my fingers run across the marble plaque, then closed my eyes to let the fact sink in. I was as close as I would ever be to the body of Christophe—Henry I, King of Haiti.

I knew the man. I had read about him in my history books as do all Haitian schoolchildren; but that was not why I felt close to him, why I wanted to be closer. More than a hero, he was a friend of the family. My father and my uncle talked about him by the hour when I was still a child. They were often critical, for reasons I did not always understand; but they were also proud of him. They both belonged to The Society of King Christophe's Friends, a small intellectual fraternity that included Aimé Césaire and Alejo Carpentier—people I knew to be famous. Back then, I thought of the society as something of a fan club engaged in secret medieval rites. I found out later that I was not entirely wrong. As playwrights, novelists, and historians, the writer-friends of Henry Christophe were alchemists of memory, proud guardians of a past that they neither lived nor wished to have shared.

The mass of the Citadel towering over me, I stood alone in the Place d'Armes, my eyes still closed, summoning images too bright to settle in the late morning sun. I tried to recall the face of Henry at various stages of his life. I had seen many pictures of him, but none of them came back. All I could reach for here were this stone and the cold cannonballs scattered a few feet away in the courtyard. I reached further into myself. Relics danced behind my eyelids in fleeting shapes and colors: the royal star of St. Henry, a medal that my father handled, a green costume, a monochrome of the royal saber, an old coin I once touched, a carriage I once imagined. These were the things of which my memory of Christophe was made but they were failing me when I most needed them.

I opened my eyes to the securing sight of the Citadel standing tall against the sky. Memories are made of stone, and Henry I built more than his share of forts and palaces so that we could come visit him. Walking over to the edge of the terrace, I surveyed the kingdom as he imagined it: the fields, the roads, the past in the present; and below, right below the clouds, the royal walls of Sans Souci, the King's favorite residence.

Sans Souci: The Palace

In the northern mountains of the Republic of Haiti, there is an old palace called Sans Souci that many urbanites and neighboring peasants revere as one of the most important historical monuments of their country. The palace—what remains of it—stands on a small elevation between the higher hills surrounding the town of Milot. It is impressive if only because of its size—or what one can now guess to have been its size. It was built to instill a long lasting deference, and it still does. One does not stumble upon these ruins; they are both too remote and too often mentioned within Haiti for the encounter to be fully accidental. Anyone who comes here, enticed by the posters of Haiti's Département du Tourisme or by one or another narrative of glory, is at least vaguely familiar with Haiti's record and assumes history to be dormant within these crumbling walls. Anyone who comes here knows that this huge dwelling was built in the early nineteenth century, for a black king, by blacks barely out of slavery. Thus the traveler is soon caught between the sense of desolation that molds Sans Souci's present and a furtive awareness of bygone glory. There is so little here to see and so much to infer. Anyone who comes here comes too late, after a climax of which little has been preserved, yet early enough to dare imagine what it might have been.

What it might have been is not left entirely to the visitor's imagination. Soon enough a peasant of the area will force himself upon you and serve as your impromptu guide. He will take you through the ruins and, for a small fee, will talk about Sans Souci.

Henry I, King of Haiti, by British painter Richard Evans

He will tell you that the palace was built by Henry Christophe, a hero of the Haitian Revolution who fought against slavery and became King of Haiti soon after the French defeat and the 1804 independence. He may or not mention that Haiti was then cut into two states with Christophe ruling the northern one. He may or not know that Millot [*sic*] was an old French plantation that Christophe took over and managed for some time during the revolution; but he will surely relate the fabulous feasts that went on at Sans Souci when Christophe became king, the opulent dinners, the dances, the brilliant costumes. He might tell you that the price was heavy, in currency and in human blood: the King was both rich and ruthless. Hundreds of Haitians died building his favorite residence, its surrounding town, and the neighboring Citadel Henry, either because of the harsh labor conditions or because they faced the firing squad for a minor breach of discipline. At this point, you may start wondering if Sans Souci was worth the price. But the peasant will continue describing the property. He will dwell on its immense gardens now denuded, its dependencies now gone, and especially its waterworks: its artificial springs and the hidden channels that were directed through the walls, supposedly to cool the castle during the summer. In the words of an old hand who took me around the ruins: "Christophe made water flow within these walls." If your guide is seasoned enough, he will preserve his main effect until the very end: having seduced your imagination, he will conclude with a touch of pride that this extravagance was meant to impress the *blan* (whites/foreigners), meant to provide the world with irrefutable evidence of the ability of the black race.[1]

On these and many other points, the printed record—the pictures and the words left behind by those who saw Sans Souci and the town of Milot before the 1842 earthquake that precipitated its ruin—corroborates the crux of the peasant's story and some of its amazing details. Geographer Karl Ritter, who drew a sketch of the palace a few days after Christophe's death, found it "very impressive to the eye." British visitor John Candler, who saw a deserted building he judged to be in poor style, admitted that it must have been "splendid" in Christophe's time. U.S. physician Jonathan Brown wrote that Sans Souci had "the reputation of having been one of the most magnificent edifices of the West Indies." Writers also preserved passing descriptions of the waterworks: Christophe did not make water flow within the walls, but Sans Souci did have an artificial spring and numerous waterworks. Similarly, the King's ruthless reputation is well established in books, some of which were written by his contemporaries; professional historians are uncertain only about the actual number of laborers who died during the construction of the palace. Christophe's racial pride is also well known: it exudes from what remains of his correspondence; it has inspired Caribbean writers from Martiniquan playwright and poet Aimé Césaire to Cuban novelist Alejo Carpentier. Long before this pride was fictionalized, one of Christophe's closest advisers, Baron Valentin de Vastey, chancellor of the kingdom, evoked the 1813 completion of Sans Souci and the adjacent Royal Church of Milot in grandiose terms that anticipated Afrocentrism by more than a century: "These two structures, erected by descendants of Africans, show that we have not lost the architectural taste and genius of our ancestors who covered Ethiopia, Egypt, Carthage, and old Spain with their superb monuments."[2]

Though the written record and the oral history transmitted by the local guides match quite closely on most substantial points, there is one topic of importance on which the peasants remain more evasive. If asked about the name of the palace, even a neophyte guide will reply, quite correctly, that "san sousi" means "carefree" in Haitian (as "sans souci" does in French) and that the words are commonly used to qualify someone who worries about little. Some may even add that the expression aptly describes the King himself, or at least the side of him that sought relaxation and the easy life of Sans Souci. Others may recall that, during Christophe's reign, the name of Sans Souci was extended to the town newly built around the palace, now a rural burg more often referred to as Milot. But few guides are prone to volunteer that "Sans Souci" was also the name of a man and that this man was killed by Henry Christophe himself.

The War Within the War

The circumstances surrounding the death of Sans Souci, the man, are often mentioned—though always in passing and rarely in detail—in historical works dealing with the Haitian war of independence. The main story line of the Haitian Revolution, which augured the end of American slavery and eventuated in the birth of Haiti from the ashes of French Saint-Domingue, will receive only a summary treatment here. In August 1791, slaves in northern Saint-Domingue launched an uprising that spread throughout the colony and turned into a successful revolution that toppled both slavery and the French colonial order. The revolution took nearly thirteen years to unfold from the initial uprising to the proclamation of Haitian independence in January 1804.

Key markers along that path are successive concessions made by France and the increasing political and military achievements of the revolutionary slaves under the leadership of a Creole black, Toussaint Louverture. In 1794, France's formal abolition of slavery recognized the freedom *de facto* gained by the slaves in arms. Soon after, Louverture moved under the French banner with his troops. From 1794 to 1798, he fought the Spaniards, who controlled the eastern part of the island, and helped the French counter an invasion by British forces. By 1797, the black general had become the most influential political and military figure in French Saint-Domingue. His "colonial" army, composed mainly of former slaves, at times numbered more than twenty thousand men. In 1801, his successful invasion of the Spanish part of Hispaniola gave him control over the entire island. Although Louverture ruled in the name of France, he promulgated an independent Constitution that recognized him as Governor-for-life with absolute power.

Revolutionary France had followed these developments with great concern. Many in the metropolis and most whites in the colony were waiting for the first opportunity to reestablish the old order. That chance came with the Consulate. First Consul Napoleon Bonaparte took advantage of the relative calm that followed his coup d'état of 18 Brumaire to prepare an expedition with secret instructions to reestablish slavery in Saint-Domingue. The historical sketch that most concerns us, which lasted less than one year, starts with the 1802 landing of the French forces.

The French expedition was led by no less than Pauline Bonaparte's husband, General Charles Leclerc, Napoleon's brother-in-law. When Leclerc reached Saint-Domingue, one key figure of Louverture's army in the north of the country, the man responsible for Cap Français, the most important town of the colony, was General Henry Christophe. Born in neighboring Grenada, a free man long before the 1791 uprising, Christophe had an unusually broad life experience for a black man of that time; he had been, in turn, a scullion, a major-domo, and a hotel manager. He had been slightly wounded in Georgia, at the battle of Savannah, while fighting on the side of the American revolutionaries in the Comte d'Estaing's regiment. When the French forces reached the port of Cap, Leclerc promptly sent Christophe a written ultimatum threatening to invade the town with fifteen thousand troops if the blacks did not surrender by daybreak. The letter Christophe wrote to Leclerc was characteristic of the man: "If you have the means with which you threaten me, I shall offer you all the resistance worthy of a general; and if fate favors your weapons, you will not enter the town of Cap until I reduce it to ashes and, then and there, I shall keep on fighting you."[3]

Then, Christophe set fire to his own sumptuous house and prepared his troops for combat.

After a few months of bloody engagements, Leclerc's forces broke down many of the revolutionaries' defenses. Henry Christophe surrendered and joined the French forces in April 1802. Soon after Christophe's defection, other prominent black officers (including Louverture's most important second, General Jean-Jacques Dessalines) also joined the French forces, quite probably with Louverture's consent. In early May 1802, Louverture himself capitulated. Even though a number of former slaves rejected that cease-fire and maintained isolated pockets of armed resistance, Leclerc used the limited calm to entrap the black general. Louverture was captured in June 1802 and sent to jail in France.

Armed resistance had not stopped completely with the successive submissions of Christophe, Dessalines, and Louverture. It escalated after Louverture's exile, especially when Leclerc ordered the disarmament of all former slaves who did not belong to the colonial regiments now formally integrated within his army. Many former slaves, now free cultivators or soldiers, had seen in Louverture's arrest a testimony of Leclerc's treachery. They viewed the disarmament decree as additional proof that the French intended to reestablish slavery. They joined the resistance in increasing numbers in August and September 1802. By October, most of the Louverture followers who had formally accepted Leclerc's authority the previous summer rejoined the resistance with their troops. These black officers forged a new alliance with light-skinned free coloreds who until then had supported the expedition. By November 1802, Dessalines had become the leader of the alliance with the blessing of the most prominent of the free coloreds, mulatto general Alexandre Pétion, a former member of Leclerc's army. A year later, the reconstituted revolutionary troops gained full control of the colony, the French acknowledged defeat, and Haiti became an independent country with Dessalines as its first chief of state.

Historians generally agree on most of these facts, with the Haitians usually insisting on the courage of their ancestors, and the foreigners—especially white foreigners—usually emphasizing the role of yellow fever in weakening the French troops. Both groups mention only in passing that the Haitian war of independence involved more than two camps. The army first put together by Toussaint Louverture and reconstituted by Dessalines did not only fight against the French expeditionary forces. At crucial moments of the war, black officers turned also against their own, engaging into what was, in effect, *a* war within *the* war.

The series of events that I call the "war within the war" stretches from about June 1802 to mid-1803. It comprises mainly two major campaigns: 1) the one led by the black officers reintegrated under Leclerc's command against the former slaves who had refused to surrender to the French (June 1802–October 1802); and 2) the one led by the same generals and the free colored officers associated with Pétion against the former slaves who refused to acknowledge the revolutionary hierarchy and the supreme authority of Dessalines (November 1802–April 1803). Crucial to the story is the fact that in both campaigns the leaders are mainly black Creoles (i.e., natives of the island, or of the Caribbean) and the dissident groups are composed of—and led by—Bossales (i.e., African-born) ex-slaves, mainly from the Congo. The story of Jean-Baptiste Sans Souci ties together these two campaigns.

Sans Souci: The Man

Colonel Jean-Baptiste Sans Souci was a Bossale slave, probably from the Congo, who played an important role in the Haitian Revolution from the very first days of the 1791 uprising. He may have obtained his name from a *quartier* called Sans Souci, which bordered the parishes of Vallières and Grande Rivière.[4] At any rate, it is in that area that we first find him in the written record. Gros, a petty French official captured by the slaves in October 1791, identified Sans Souci as the rebel commander of the camp the slaves had set up on the Cardinaux plantation in Grande Rivière. The prisoner seemed to know of the man, whom he described only as a black slave and "a very bad lot" (*très mauvais sujet*). However, since Gros stayed only one night in Cardinaux before being moved to another plantation seized by the ex-slaves, he does not provide any details about this camp or its commander.[5]

We know from other sources that Sans Souci remained active within the same area. Like other Congo military leaders, he excelled at the guerrilla-type tactics, reminiscent of the Congo civil wars of the eighteenth century, which were critical to the military evolution of the Haitian Revolution.[6] After Toussaint Louverture unified the revolutionary forces, Sans Souci maintained his influence and became one of Henry Christophe's immediate subalterns. At the time of the French invasion, he was military commander of the *arrondissement* of Grande Rivière, then an important military district in the north of Saint-Domingue that included his original Cardinaux camp. Between February and April 1802 he repeatedly won out over the French expeditionary forces in the areas he controlled. Like many other black officers, he tacitly accepted Leclerc's victory after Louverture's surrender. I do not know of a document indicating Sans Souci's formal submission, but for the month of June at least, the French referred to him by his colonial grade—which suggests his integration within Leclerc's military organization.

Sans Souci's formal presence in the French camp was quite short—lasting less than a month. Leclerc, who had reports that the Colonel was covertly reorganizing the colonial troops and calling on cultivators to join a new rebellion, gave a secret order for his arrest on July 4, 1802. French general Philibert Fressinet, a veteran of Napoleon's Italian campaigns (then, nominally at least, the superior of both Christophe and Sans Souci who were technically French colonial officers), took steps to implement that order. But Sans Souci did not wait for Fressinet. He defected with most of his troops, launching a vigorous attack on a neighboring French camp on July 7. Fressinet then wrote to Leclerc: "I am warning you, General, that *le nommé* [the so-called] Sans Souci has just rebelled and tries to win to his party as many cultivators as he can. He is even now encircling the Cardinio [Cardinaux] camp. General Henry Christophe is marching against him."[7]

Between early July and November, troops from both the colonial and expeditionary forces, led in turn by Christophe, Dessalines, and Fressinet himself, among others, tried unsuccessfully to overpower Sans Souci. The African, meanwhile, gained the loyalty of other blacks, soldiers and cultivators alike. He soon became the leader of a substantial army, at least one powerful enough to give constant concern to the French. Using primarily guerrilla-type tactics, Sans Souci exploited his greater knowledge of the topography and his troops' better adaptation to the local environment to keep at bay both the French and the colonial forces still affiliated with Leclerc. While Christophe, Pétion, and Dessalines managed to subdue other foci of resistance, the extreme mobility of Sans Souci's small units made it impossible to dislodge him from his moving retreats in the northern mountains.[8]

By early September 1802, Leclerc ordered French general Jean Boudet to launch an all-out effort against Sans Souci with the backing of French general Jean-Baptiste Brunet and Dessalines himself, then recognized by the French as the most capable of the Creole higher ranks. Brunet alone led three thousand troops. Sans Souci's riposte was brisk and fierce. Commenting soon after on the massive offensive of 15 September, Leclerc wrote to Napoleon: "This day alone cost me 400 men." By the end of September Sans Souci and his most important allies, Makaya and Sylla, had nearly reversed the military situation in the northern part of the country. They never occupied any lowland territory for long, if at all; but they made it impossible for the French troops and their Creole allies to do so securely.[9]

The sustained resistance of various dissident groups (composed mainly of Africans—among whom those controlled or influenced by Sans Souci were the most important) and their continuous harassment of the French created an untenable situation for both Leclerc and the Creole officers under his command. On the one hand, an ailing and exasperated Leclerc (he died before the end of the war) took much less care to hide his ultimate plan: the deportation of most black and mulatto officers and the restoration of slavery. On the other hand, the Creole officers, constantly suspected by the French to be in connivance with Sans Souci or other leaders of the resistance, found themselves under increasing pressure to defect. By November 1802, most colonial officers had turned once more against the French, and Dessalines was acknowledged as the military leader of the new alliance forged between himself, Pétion, and Christophe.

But just as some former slaves had refused to submit to the French, some (often the same) contested the new revolutionary hierarchy. Jean-Baptiste Sans Souci notably declined the new leaders' repeated invitations to join ranks with them, arguing that his own unconditional resistance to the French exempted him from obedience to his former superiors. He would not serve under men whose allegiance to the cause of freedom was, at the very least, dubious; and he especially resented Christophe whom he considered a traitor. It is in this second phase of the war within the war that Sans Souci marched to his death. Within a few weeks, the Creole generals defeated or won out over most of the dissidents. Sans Souci resisted longer than most but eventually agreed to negotiations with Dessalines, Pétion, and Christophe about his role in the new hierarchy. At one of these meetings, he virtually assured Dessalines that he would recognize his supreme authority, thus in effect reversing his dissidence but without appearing to bow to Christophe personally. Still, Christophe asked for one more meeting with his former subaltern. Sans Souci showed up at Christophe's headquarters on the Grand Pré plantation with only a small guard. He and his followers fell under the bayonets of Christophe's soldiers.

Sans Souci's existence and death are mentioned in most written accounts of the Haitian war of independence. Likewise, professional historians who deal with Christophe's rule always note the king's fondness for grandiose constructions and his predilection for the Milot palace, his favorite residence. But few writers have puzzled over the palace's peculiar name. Fewer have commented on the obvious: that its name and the patronym of the man killed by Christophe ten years before the erection of his royal residence are the same. Even fewer have noted, let alone emphasized, that there were three, rather than two, "Sans Soucis": the man and two palaces. Six decades before Christophe's coronation, Prussian Emperor Frederick the Great had built himself a grandiose palace on top of a hill in the town of Potsdam, a few miles from Berlin. That palace, a *haut-lieu* of the European Enlightenment, which some observers claim to have been part inspiration for the purpose—and perhaps the architectural design—of Milot, was called Sans Souci.

Sans Souci Revisited

With their various layers of silences, the three faces of Sans Souci provide numerous vantage points from which to examine the means and process of historical production. Concrete reminders that the uneven power of historical production is expressed also through the power to touch, to see, and to feel, they span a material continuum that goes from the solidity of Potsdam to the missing body of the Colonel. They also provide us with a concrete example of the interplay between inequalities in the historical process and inequalities in the historical narrative, an interplay which starts long before the historian (qua collector, narrator, or interpreter) comes to the scene.

Romantic reevaluation of the weak and defeated notwithstanding, the starting points are different. Sans Souci–Potsdam is knowable in ways that Sans Souci–Milot will never be. The Potsdam palace is still standing. Its mass of stone and mortar has retained most of its shape and weight, and it is still furnished with what passes for the best of rococo elegance. Indeed, Frederick's successor started its historical maintenance, its transformation into an archive of a sort, by reconstructing Frederick's room the very year of Frederick's death. Frederick's own body, in his well-kept coffin, has become a marker of German history. Hitler stood at his Potsdam grave to proclaim the Third Reich. Devoted German officers removed the coffin from Potsdam as the Soviet army moved into Berlin. Chancellor Kohl had the coffin reinterred in the Potsdam garden in the early 1990s as a tribute to—and symbol of—German reunification. Frederick has been reburied beside his beloved dogs. Two centuries after Frederick's death, both he and his palace have a materiality that history needs both to explain and to acknowledge.

In contrast to Potsdam, the Milot palace is a wreck. Its walls were breached by civil war, neglect, and natural disasters. They testify to a physical decline that started the very year of Christophe's death and accelerated over the years. Christophe had no political heir, certainly no immediate successor eager and able to preserve his personal quarters. He committed suicide in the midst of an uprising, and the republicans who took over his kingdom had no wish to transform Sans Souci into a monument. Although

Sans Souci–Milot, today

Christophe's stature as myth preceded his death, his full-fledged conversion into national hero came much later. Still, like Frederick, he is buried in his most famous construction, the Citadel Henry, now a UNESCO World Heritage landmark not far away from Sans Souci. The Milot palace itself has become a monument—though one which reflects both the limited means and the determination of the Haitian government and people to invest in historical preservation. In spite of the devotion of two Haitian architects, its restoration lags behind schedule, in part for lack of funds. Further, even a reconstructed Milot will not have the same claims to history as a regularly maintained historical monument, such as the palace at Potsdam. The surrounding town of Milot, in turn, has lost historical significance.

As for the body of the Colonel, it is somewhat misleading to state it as "missing," for it was never reported as such. As far as we know, no one ever claimed it, and its memory does not even live in the bodies of his descendants—if any—in or around Milot. Further, whereas we know what both Christophe and Frederick looked like because both had the wish and the power to have their features engraved for posterity, one of the three faces of Sans Souci may have disappeared forever, at least in its most material form. The royal portrait commissioned by Henry I from Richard Evans, reproduced in many recent books, remains a source that Sans Souci the man has yet to match: there is no known image of the Colonel. In short, because historical traces are inherently uneven, sources are not created equal.

But if lived inequalities yield unequal historical power, they do so in ways we have yet to determine. The distribution of historical power does not necessarily replicate the inequalities (victories and setbacks, gains and losses) lived by the actors. Historical power is not a direct reflection of a past occurrence, or a simple sum of past inequalities measured from an actor's perspective or from the standpoint of any "objective" standard, even at the first moment. The French superiority in artillery, the strategic superiority of Sans Souci, and the political superiority of Christophe can all be demonstrated, but no such demonstration would enable us to predict their relative significance then and now. Similarly, sources do not encapsulate the whole range of significance of the occurrences to which they testify.

Further, the outcome itself does not determine in any linear way how an event or a series of events enters into history. The French expeditionary forces lost the Haitian war. (They thought they did, and they did.) Similarly, Colonel Sans Souci was the loser and Christophe the ultimate winner both politically and militarily within the black camp. Yet the papers preserved by General Donatien Rochambeau (Leclerc's successor as commander of the

French expedition) show more than fifty entries about French general Fressinet in spite of the fact that Fressinet was, by anyone's standard, a fairly minor figure in the Saint-Domingue campaigns. In comparison, there are eleven entries about Christophe, whom we know gave both Leclerc and Rochambeau much more to think about than Fressinet ever did. Sans Souci, in turn—who came close to upsetting the plans of both the French and colonial officers and indeed forced both to change tactics in mid-course—received a single entry.[10]

Thus the presences and absences embodied in sources (artifacts and bodies that turn an event into fact) or archives (facts collected, thematized, and processed as documents and monuments) are neither neutral or natural. They are created. As such, they are not mere presences and absences, but mentions or silences of various kinds and degrees. By silence, I mean an active and transitive process: one "silences" a fact or an individual as a silencer silences a gun. One engages in the practice of silencing. Mentions and silences are thus active, dialectical counterparts of which history is the synthesis. Almost every mention of Sans Souci, the palace, the very resilience of the physical structure itself, effectively silences Sans Souci, the man, his political goals, his military genius.

Inequalities experienced by the actors lead to uneven historical power in the inscription of traces. Sources built upon these traces in turn privilege some events over others, not always the ones privileged by the actors. Sources are thus instances of inclusion, the other face of which is, of course, what is excluded. This may now be obvious enough to those of us who have learned (though more recently than we care to remember) that sources imply choices. But the conclusion we tend to draw that some occurrences have the capacity (a physical one, I would insist) to enter history and become "fact" at the first stage while others do not is much too general, and ultimately useless in its ecumenical form. That some peoples and things are absent of history, lost, as it were, to the possible world of knowledge, is much less relevant to the historical practice than the fact that some peoples and things are absent in history, and that this absence itself is constitutive of the process of historical production.

Silences are inherent in history because any single event enters history with some of its constituting parts missing. Something is always left out while something else is recorded. There is no perfect closure of any event, however one chooses to define the boundaries of that event. Thus whatever becomes fact does so with its own inborn absences, specific to its production. In other words, the very mechanisms that make any historical recording possible also ensure that historical facts are not created equal. They reflect differential control of the means of historical production at the very first engraving that transforms an event into a fact.[11] Silences of this kind show the limits of strategies that imply a more accurate reconstitution of the past, and therefore the production of a "better" history, simply by an enlargement of the empirical base.[12] To be sure, the continuous enlargement of the physical boundaries of historical production is useful and necessary. The turn toward hitherto neglected sources (e.g., diaries, images, bodies) and the emphasis on unused facts (e.g., facts of gender, race, and class, facts of the life cycle, facts of resistance) are pathbreaking developments. My point is that when these tactical gains are made to dictate strategy they lead, at worst, to a neo-empiricist enterprise and, at best, to an unnecessary restriction of the battleground for historical power.

As sources fill the historical landscape with their facts, they reduce the room available to other facts. Even if we imagine the landscape to be forever expandable, the rule of interdependence implies that new facts cannot emerge in a vacuum. They will have to gain their right to existence in light of the field constituted by previously created facts. They may dethrone some of these facts, erase or qualify others. The point remains that sources occupy competing positions in the historical landscape. These positions themselves are inherently imbued with meaning since facts cannot be created meaningless. Even as an ideal recorder, the chronicler necessarily produces meaning and, therefore, silences.

The tenets of the distinction between chronicler and narrator are well known.[13] The chronicler provides a play-by-play account of every event he witnesses, the narrator describes the life of an entity, person, thing, or institution. The chronicler deals with discrete chunks of time united only by his record-keeping; the narrator deals with a continuity provided by the life span of the entity described. The chronicler describes only events that he witnessed; the narrator can tell stories both about what he saw and what he learned to be true from others. The chronicler does not know the end of the story—indeed, there is no point to the story; the narrator knows the full story. The speech of the chronicler is akin to that of a radio announcer giving a play-by-play account of a sports game; the speech of the narrator is akin to that of a storyteller.[14]

Even if we admit that distinction as couched, silences are inherent in the chronicle. The sportscaster's account is a play-by-play description but only of the occurrences that matter to the game. Even if it is guided mainly by the seriality of occurrences, it tends to leave out from the series witnesses, participants, and events considered generally as marginal. The audience enters primarily when it is seen as influencing the players. Players on the bench are left out. Players in the field are mentioned mainly when they capture the ball, or at least when they try to capture it or are meant to do so. Silences are necessary to the account, for if the sportscaster told us every "thing" that happened at each and every moment, we would not understand anything. If the account was indeed fully comprehensive of all facts it would be incomprehensible. Further, the selection of what matters, the dual creation of mentions and silences, is premised on the understanding of the rules of the game by broadcaster and audience alike. In short, play-by-play accounts are restricted in terms of what may enter them and in terms of the order in which these elements may enter.

What is true of play-by-play accounts is no less true of notary records, business accounts, population censuses, parish registers. Historians familiar with the plantation records that inscribe the daily life of Caribbean slaves are well aware that births are underreported in these records.[15] Planters or overseers often preferred not to register the existence of a black baby whose survival was unlikely, given the high incidence of infant mortality. Temporary omission made more sense: it could be corrected if the child survived beyond a certain age.

We are not dealing here with a case in which technical or ideological blinders skewed the reporting of the chronicler. It is not as if these lives and deaths were missed by negligence. Nor were they inconsequential to the chronicler: pregnancies and births considerably affected the amount of available labor, the linchpin of the slave system. Masters were not even trying to conceal these births. Rather, both births and deaths were actively silenced in the records for a combination of practical reasons inherent in the reporting itself. To be sure, slavery and racism provided the context within which these silences occurred, but in no way were the silences themselves the direct products of ideology. They made sense in terms of the reporting, in terms of the logic of its accounting procedures. In short, the chronicler-accountant is no less passive than the chronicler-sportscaster. As Emile Benveniste reminds us, the census taker is always a *censor*—and not only because of a lucky play of etymology: he who counts heads always silences facts and voices.[16] Silences are inherent in the creation of sources, the first moment of historical production.

Unequal control over historical production obtains also in the second moment of historical production, the making of archives and documents. Of course, sources and documents can emerge simultaneously and some analysts conflate the two.[17] My own insistence on distinguishing a moment of fact-assembly from that of fact-creation is meant first to emphasize that uneven historical power obtains even before any work of classification by non-participants. Slave plantation records entered history as sources with the added value of the inequalities that made them possible long before they were classified into archives. Second, I want to insist that the kind of power used in the creation of sources is not necessarily the same that allows the creation of archives.[18]

By archives, I mean the institutions that organize facts and sources and condition the possibility of existence of historical statements. Archival power determines the difference between a historian, amateur or professional, and a charlatan.

Archives assemble. Their assembly work is not limited to a more or less passive act of collecting. Rather, it is an active act of production that prepares facts for historical intelligibility. Archives set up both the substantive and formal elements of the narrative. They are the institutionalized sites of mediation between the sociohistorical process and the narrative about that process. They enforce the constraints on "debatability" we noted earlier with Appadurai: they convey authority and set the rules for credibility and interdependence; they help select the stories that matter.

So conceived, the category covers competing institutions with various conditions of existence and various modes of labor organization. It includes not only the libraries or depositories sponsored by states and foundations, but less visible institutions that also sort sources to organize facts, according to themes or periods, into documents to be used and monuments to be explored. In that sense, a tourist guide, a museum tour, an archaeological expedition, or an auction at Sotheby's can perform as much an archival role as the Library of Congress.[19] The historical guild or, more properly, the rules that condition academic history perform similar archival duties. These rules enforce constraints that belie the romantic image of the professional historian as an independent artist or isolated artisan. The historian is never alone even within the most obscure corner of the archive: the encounter with the document is also an encounter with the guild even for the amateur.

In short, the making of archives involves a number of selective operations: selection of producers, selection of evidence, selection of themes, selection of procedures—which means, at best the differential ranking and, at worst, the exclusion of some producers, some evidence, some themes, some procedures. Power enters here both obviously and surreptitiously. Jean-Baptiste Sans Souci was silenced not only because some narrators may have consciously chosen not to mention him but primarily because most writers followed the acknowledged rules of their time.

Silences in the Historical Narrative

The dialectics of mentions and silences obtain also at the third moment of the process, when events that have become facts (and may have been processed through archives) are retrieved. Even if we assume instances of pure historical "narrativity," that is, accounts that describe an alleged past in a way analogous to a sportscaster's play-by-play description of a game, even if we postulate a recording angel—with no stakes in the story—who would dutifully note all that was mentioned and collected, any subsequent narrative (or any corpus of such narratives) would demonstrate to us that retrieval and recollection proceed unequally. Occurrences equally noted, and supposedly not yet subject to interpretation in the most common sense of the word, exhibit in the historical corpus an unequal frequency of retrieval, unequal (factual) weight, indeed unequal degrees of factualness. Some facts are recalled more often than others; some strings of facts are recalled with more empirical richness than others even in play-by-play accounts.

Every fact recorded in my narrative of the Sans Souci story is part of the available record in relatively accessible form since I have used only sources available in multiple copies: memoirs, published accounts, so-called "secondary" sources—that is, material already produced as history. But the frequency with which they appear in the total corpus from which the narrative was drawn varies. So does the material weight of mention, that is, the sheer empirical value of the string within which any single fact is enmeshed.

That Colonel Sans Souci was not the leader of an impromptu or marginal rebel band but an early leader in the slave uprising and, later, a high-ranking officer of Louverture's army turned dissident has been a constant fact within the published record from the late eighteenth century to our times.[20] But that fact remained largely unused until recently: its frequency of retrieval was low, its empirical elaboration defective in terms of the information already available in that corpus. Sans Souci was most often alluded to without mention of grade or origins, without even a first name, all available facts within the corpus. Little was said of the size of his troops, of the details of his death, of his few stated positions.[21] Yet there was enough to sketch a picture of Sans Souci, even if a very fleeting one, certainly not as elaborate as that of Christophe.

Still, materials of that sort had to re-enter the corpus, so to speak, quite slowly and in restricted ways—for instance, as part of a catalogue of documents within which they remained more or less inconspicuous.[22] Only in the 1980s have they surfaced as (re)discoveries in their own right within a narrative.[23] Thus, to many readers who had access to most of this corpus and who may or may not have different stakes in the narrative, the extent of Sans Souci's political dissidence—if not that of his existence—is likely to be apprehended as "news." So is (for a different group of readers, overlapping—and as substantial as—the first one) the suggestion that the palace at Milot may have been modeled after the palace at Potsdam to an extent still undetermined.

Now, the individuals who constructed this corpus came from various times and backgrounds, sought to offer various interpretations of the Haitian Revolution, and passed at times opposite value judgments on either the revolution itself or Christophe. Given these conflicting viewpoints, what explains the greater frequency of certain silences in the corpus?

Let us go back to the actual practice of an Ideal Chronicler. Our description of that practice suggests that play-by-play accounts and even inventory lists are restricted, not only in terms of the occurrences they register, but also in terms of the order in which these occurrences are registered. In other words, no chronicle can avoid a minimal structure of narration, a movement that gives it some sense. That structure, barely visible in the typical chronicle, becomes fundamental to the narrative proper.

Historical narratives are premised on previous understandings, which are themselves premised on the distribution of archival power. In the case of Haitian historiography, as in the case of most Third World countries, these previous understandings have been profoundly shaped by Western conventions and procedures. First, the writing and reading of Haitian historiography implies literacy and formal access to a Western—primarily French—language and culture, two prerequisites that already exclude the majority of Haitians from direct participation in its production. Most Haitians are illiterate and unilingual speakers of Haitian, a French-based Creole. Only a few members of the already tiny elite are native bilingual speakers of French and Haitian. The first published memoirs and histories of the revolution were written almost exclusively in French. So were most of the written traces (letters, proclamations) that have become primary documents. Currently, the vast majority of history books about Saint-

Domingue/Haiti is written in French, with a substantial minority of those published in France itself. The first full-length history book (and for that matter the first full-length non-fiction book) written in Haitian Creole is my own work on the revolution, which dates from 1977.[24]

Second, regardless of their training and the degree to which they may be considered members of a guild, Haitian and foreign narrators aim to conform to guild practice. The division between guild historians and amateurs is, of course, premised on a particular Western-dominated practice. In the Haitian case, few if any individuals make a living writing history. Haitian historians have included physicians, lawyers, journalists, businessmen, bureaucrats and politicians, high school teachers and clergymen. Status as historian is not conferred by an academic doctoral degree but by a mixture of publications that conform to a large extent to the standards of the Western guild and active participation in ongoing historical debates. Previous understandings here include an acknowledgment of the now global academic division of labor as shaped by the particular history of Western Europe. Just as sportscasters assume an audience's limited knowledge of the players (who is who, what are the two sides), so do historians build their narrative on the shoulders of previous ones. The knowledge that narrators assume about their audience limits both their use of the archives and the context within which their story finds significance. To contribute to new knowledge and to add new significance, the narrator must both acknowledge and contradict the power embedded in previous understandings.

This chapter itself exemplifies the point. My narrative of the Haitian Revolution assumed both a certain way of reading history and the reader's greater knowledge of French than of Haitian history. Whether or not these assumptions were correct, they reflect a presumption about the unevenness of historical power. But if they were correct, the narrative had to present an overview of the last years of the Haitian Revolution. Otherwise, the story of Sans Souci would not make sense to most readers. I did not feel the need to underscore that Haiti is in the Caribbean and that Afro-American slavery had been going on in the Caribbean for exactly three centuries when these events occurred. These mentions would have added to the empirical weight of the narrative, but the story still made sense without them. Further, I assumed that most of my readers knew these facts. Still, expecting many of my readers to be North American undergraduates, I took the precaution of inserting throughout the text some clues about Haiti's topography and its general history. I did not report that Toussaint's capture (which I qualified as an entrapment) occurred on June 7, 1802, because the exact date did not seem to matter much in the narrative. But if I had done so I would have used, as I do now, the Christian calendar, the year indexation system the West inherited from Dionysius Exiguus rather than, say, an oriental system. Nowhere in this text do I use the *calendrier républicain* (the system that indexed months and years in most of the primary documents of this story) because it did not prevail in post-revolutionary narratives and lost, therefore, its archival power. Even individuals who were forced to learn its correspondence with Dionysius's system at an early age (as I was in school) would take some time to ascertain that "le 18 prairial de l'an dix" was indeed June 7, 1802. In short, I bowed to some rules, inherited from a history of uneven power, to ensure the accessibility of my narrative.

Thus, in many ways, my account followed a conventional line—but only up to a certain point because of my treatment of Sans Souci. Until now indeed, the combined effect of previous understandings about plot structures and common empirical knowledge resulted in a partial silencing of the life and death of the Colonel. Players have been distributed according to the major leagues, and the event-units of Haitian history have been cut in slices that cannot be easily modified. Thus the war within the war has been subsumed within accounts of the war between the French and the colonial troops, rarely (if ever) detailed as a narrative in its own right. In that sense, indeed, it never constituted a complete sequence, a play-by-play account of any "thing." Rather, its constituting events were retrieved as marginal subparts of other accounts, and the life and death of Sans Souci himself as a smaller segment of these subparts. To unearth Colonel Sans Souci as more than a negligible figure within the story of Haiti's emergence, I chose to add a section that recast his story as a separate account after the chronological sketch of the revolution. This was a choice based on both possible procedures and assessment of my readers' knowledge. That choice acknowledges power, but it also introduces some dissidence by setting up the war within the war as a historical topic.

To be sure, I could have highlighted the figure of the Colonel in a different way. But I had to resort to a procedure of emphasis based on both content and form in order to reach my final goal, that of suggesting new significance to both the Haitian Revolution and to the Colonel's life. I could not leave to chance the transformation of some silences into mentions or the possibility that mentions alone would add retrospective significance. In short, this unearthing of Sans Souci required extra labor not so much in the production of new facts but in their transformation into a new narrative.

Silences Within Silences

The unearthing of silences, and the historian's subsequent emphasis on the retrospective significance of hitherto neglected events, requires not only extra labor at the archives—whether or not one uses primary sources—but also a project linked to an interpretation. This is so because the combined silences accrued through the first three steps of the process of historical production intermesh and solidify at the fourth and final moment when retrospective significance itself is produced. To call this moment "final" does not suggest that it follows the chronological disappearance of the actors. Retrospective significance can be created by the actors themselves, as a past within their past, or as a future within their present. Henry I killed Sans Souci twice: first, literally, during their last meeting; second, symbolically, by naming his most famous palace Sans Souci. This killing in history was as much for his benefit as it was for our wonder. It erased Sans Souci from Christophe's own past, and it erased him from his future, what has become the historians' present. It did not erase Sans Souci from Christophe's memory or even from the sources. Historian Hénock Trouillot, one of the few Haitians to emphasize the similarity between the two names, suggests that Christophe may even have wanted to perpetuate the memory of his enemy as the most formidable one he defeated. In other words, the silencing of Sans Souci could be read as an engraving of Christophe himself, the ultimate victor over all mortal enemies and over death itself:

> In erecting Sans Souci at the foothills of Milot, did Christophe want to prove how solidly his power was implanted in this soil? Or else, was he dominated by a more obscure thought? For a legend reports that a diviner foretold Christophe that he would die by the hand of a Congo. Then, superstitious as he was, having satisfied his propensity for magic, did he believe that in erecting this town he could defy destiny? . . . We do not know.[25]

The suggestion is not far-fetched. That Christophe deemed himself one notch above most mortals was well known even in his lifetime. Further, his reliance on transformative rituals, his desire to control both humans and death itself are epitomized in his last moments. Having engaged unsuccessfully in various rituals to restore his failing health and knowing that he had lost the personal magnetism that made his contemporaries tremble at his sight, a paralyzed Christophe shot himself, reportedly with a silver bullet, before a growing crowd of insurgents reached Sans Souci. Whether that bullet was meant to save him from a Congo, as such, we do not know.

But we know that the silencing was effective, that Sans Souci's life and death have been endowed with only marginal retrospective significance while neither Christophe's apologists nor his detractors fail to mention the king's thirst for glory and the extent to which he achieved it in his lifetime and thereafter. The legend of the diviner may one day be transformed into fact. But Trouillot's references to superstition notwithstanding, the real magic remains this dual production of a highly significant mention of glory and an equally significant silence. Christophe indeed defied the future with this silencing.

For silencing here is an erasure more effective than the absence or failure of memory, whether faked or genuine.[26] French general Pamphile de Lacroix had no particular reason to take publicly the side of either man at the time that he wrote his memoirs. He knew them both. His own life intersected with theirs in ways that usually inscribe events in memory: they were both his enemies and his subalterns at different times in a foreign war about which he was half-convinced and ended up losing. He is the only human being we know to have left records of a conversation with Christophe about Colonel Sans Souci. That sixty pages after he reports this conversation, de Lacroix mentions by name the favorite palace of Henry I without commenting on the connection between that name and the Colonel's patronym testifies to the effectiveness of Christophe's silencing.[27]

Indeed, de Lacroix's silence typifies an obliteration that may have gone beyond Christophe's wishes. For in many non-Haitian circles, the disappearance of Sans Souci the man tied the entire significance of the palace at Milot to Sans Souci–Potsdam. Jonathan Brown, the physician from New Hampshire who visited Haiti a decade after Christophe's death and failed to note the connection between the Colonel and the palace, wrote: "[Christophe] was particularly delighted with history, of which his knowledge was extensive and accurate; and Frederick the Great of Prussia was a personage with whom above all others he was captivated, the name of Sans Souci having been borrowed from Potsdam."[28]

The excerpt from Brown is one of the earliest written mentions of a relationship between the two palaces and the most likely source for subsequent writers in the English language. The only reference to Potsdam prior to Brown in the corpus covered here is buried in a diatribe against Christophe by Haitian writer and politician Hérard Dumesle. Dumesle does not say that the Milot palace was designed or named after Potsdam. Rather, he emphasizes a fundamental contradiction between what he perceives as Frederick's love of justice and Christophe's tyranny.[29] Elsewhere in the book, Dumesle also compares Christophe with Nero and Caligula. He derides Christophe's ceremonial corps of amazons who, in his view, were much less graceful than the real amazons of pre-conquest South America. In short, as mentioned by Dumesle, the connection between Potsdam and Milot is purely rhetorical. Has history turned this rhetoric into a source? Hubert Cole, who wrote an important biography of Christophe, expands on the theme of German influence on Haitian architecture of the time and claims that "German engineers" built the Citadel. Cole, like Brown, does not cite sources for his suggestions.

Implicitly contradicting Brown and Cole, Haitian historian Vergniaud Leconte credits Christophe's military engineer, Henri Barré, for the design of the Citadel and one Chéri Warloppe for the design and building of Sans Souci.[30] Leconte examined most writings then available about Christophe and claimed to have used new documents as well as oral sources, but except for locating Warloppe's grave in a cemetery in northern Haiti, he does not tie his data to specific archives or sources. Leconte does not allude to any German influence. Explicitly rejecting such influence, Haitian architect Patrick Delatour, who is involved in the restoration of the palace, insists upon viewing it within Christophe's larger project of building a royal town. For Delatour (personal communications), the foreign association—if any—is that of French urban planning at the turn of the century. Did someone dream of the German connection?

There were German—and other European—residents in Christophe's kingdom. There were Haitians fluent in German—and in other European languages—at the king's personal service.[31] Moreover, Christophe did hire German military engineers to strengthen the defenses of his kingdom. Charles Mackenzie, the British consul in Haiti and a self-avowed spy, describes the case of two of these Germans whom Christophe jailed in order to prevent them from divulging military secrets. Yet Mackenzie, who visited and described Sans Souci less than ten years after Christophe's death, does not connect the two palaces.[32]

Still, given what we know of Henry I, and given the presence of German military architects in his kingdom, it is more than probable that he was aware of Potsdam's existence and that he knew what it looked like. That Frederick contributed to the design of Sans Souci–Potsdam, wrote poetry, received in his palace celebrities of his time, men like Johann Sebastian Bach and Voltaire—also suggest an example that could have inspired Christophe. Henry I indeed supervised personally the construction of Sans Souci–Milot and maintained there the closest Haitian equivalent to an intellectual salon, thus reproducing, knowingly or not, aspects of the dream of Potsdam. None of this authenticates a

Sans Souci–Milot, a nineteenth-century engraving

strong Potsdam connection. Having compared numerous images of the two palaces, which include sketches of Sans Souci before 1842, I find that they betray some vague similarities both in general layout and in some details (the cupola of the church, the front arcades). But I will immediately confess that my amateurish associations require at least a suspicion of influence. How grounded is such a suspicion?

The strongest evidence against a strong Potsdam connection is yet another silence. Austro-German geographer Karl Ritter, a seasoned traveler and a keen observer of peoples and places, visited Sans Souci eight days after Christophe's death. Ritter climbed upon a hill and drew a picture of the palace. His text describes in detail a building that was "built entirely according to European taste" and emphasizes such features as Christophe's bathroom and the "European" plants in the garden.[33] Indeed, the word "European" returns many times in the written description, but nowhere is there the suggestion of an affinity between Christophe's residence and that of Frederick.

Ritter had the benefit of both immediacy and hindsight. Most resident foreigners had been kept away from the road to the Citadel and, therefore, from Sans Souci during Christophe's tenure. A few days after the king's suicide, some European residents rushed to discover by themselves Christophe's two most famous constructions. Ritter joined that party. Thus, he visited the palace in the company of other whites at a time when Sans Souci "triggered so much interest" among the few white residents of Haiti that "every white had to talk about it."[34]

Ritter does not report these conversations but one can presume that he took them into consideration while writing his text. At the same time, since that text was published much later, indeed after that of Dumesle and that of Mackenzie, Ritter could have picked up from either of these two writers hints to a German connection. Yet Ritter never alludes to a specifically "German" or "Prussian" influence on Sans Souci–Milot.[35] Either he never heard of it, even from fellow German speakers residing in Haiti, or he thought it inconsequential both then and later. How interesting, in light of this silence, that later writers gave Potsdam so much retrospective significance.

Hubert Cole is one of the few writers to have noted explicitly the connection between Potsdam, Milot, and Sans Souci the man, whom he identifies as a major-general. But he depreciates the link between the latter two and makes Potsdam pivotal. Cole spends a single sentence on the three faces of Sans Souci to produce a quite eloquent silence: "Here, at the foot of the Pic de la Ferrière, guarded by the fortress that he called Citadel-Henry, he built Sans-Souci, naming it out of admiration for Frederick the Great and despite the fact that it was also the name of the bitter enemy whom he had murdered."[36]

For Cole, the coincidence between Sans Souci–Milot and Sans Souci the man was an accident that the king easily bypassed. The Colonel had no symbolic significance (I am aware of being redundant in phrasing it this way), only a factual one. In retrospect, only Sans Souci–Potsdam mattered, though Cole does not say why it should matter so much. In so stressing Potsdam, Cole not only silences the Colonel, he also denies Christophe's own attempt to silence Sans Souci the man. Cole's silencing thus produces a Christophe who is a remorseless murderer, a tasteless potentate, a bare mimic of Frederick, a man who consumes his victim and appropriates his war name, not through a ritual of reckoning but by gross inadvertence.[37]

Such a picture is not convincing. A 1786 map of northern Saint-Domingue shows the main Grand Pré plantation to be adjacent to the Millot [*sic*] plantation.[38] Christophe used both places as headquarters. Given the size of the palace and its dependencies, the royal domain may have run over part of Grand Pré. In other words, Christophe built Sans Souci, the palace, a few yards away from—if not exactly—where he killed Sans Souci, the man. Coincidence and inadvertence seem quite improbable. More likely, the king was engaged in a transformative ritual to absorb his old enemy.[39]

Dahoman oral history reports that the country was founded by Tacoodonou after a successful war against Da, the ruler of Abomey. Tacoodonou "put Da to death by cutting open his belly, and placed his body under the foundation of a palace that he built in Abomey, as a memorial of his victory; which he called Dahomy, from Da the unfortunate victim, and Homy his belly: that is a house built in Da's belly."[40] The elements of the Sans Souci plot are there: the war, the killing, the building of a palace, and the naming of it after the dead enemy. Chances are that Christophe knew this story. He praised Dahomans as great warriors. He bought or recruited four thousand blacks—many of whom were reportedly from Dahomey—to bolster his army. A hundred and fifty of his Royal-Dahomets, based at Sans Souci, formed his cherished cadet troop.[41] In light of this, the emphasis on Potsdam by non-Haitian historians, which deprives the Colonel's death of any significance, is also an act of silencing.

The Defeat of the Barbarians

For Haitians, the silencing is elsewhere. To start with, Potsdam is not even a matter of fact. When I raised the issue of the influence of the German palace on the construction of Sans Souci, most of my Haitian interlocutors acknowledged ignorance. Some historians conceded that they had "heard of it," but the connection was never taken seriously. In that sense, Haitian historians are playing by the rules of the Western guild: there is no irrefutable evidence of a connection between Milot and Potsdam. But for most Haitians (most urbanites at least), the silencing goes way beyond this mere matter of fact. The literate Haitians with whom I raised the Potsdam connection did not simply question the evidence. Rather, the attitude was that, even if proven, this "fact" itself did not much matter. Just as the Colonel's name and murder—of which they are well aware—does not much matter.

For the Haitian urban elites, only Milot counts, and two of the faces of Sans Souci are ghosts that are best left undisturbed. The Colonel is for them the epitome of the war within the war, an episode that, until recently, they have denied, any retrospective significance. This fratricide sequence is the only blemish in the glorious epic of their ancestors' victory against France, the only shameful page in the history of the sole successful slave revolution in the annals of humankind. Thus, understandably, it is the one page they would have written otherwise if history depended only on the wishes of the narrator. And indeed, they tried to rewrite it as much as they could. For most writers sympathetic to the cause of freedom, Haitians and foreigners alike, the war within the war is an amalgam of unhappy incidents that pitted the black Jacobins, Creole slaves and freedmen alike, against hordes of uneducated "Congos," African-born slaves, Bossale men with strange surnames, like Sans Souci, Makaya, Sylla, Mavougou, Lamour de la Rance, Petit-Noël Prieur (or Prière), Va-Malheureux, Macaque, Alaou, Coco, Sanglaou—slave names quite distinguishable from the French sounding ones of Jean-Jacques Dessalines, Alexandre Pétion, Henry Christophe, Augustin Clervaux, and the like.

That many of these Congos were early leaders of the 1791 uprising, that a few had become bona fide officers of Louverture's army, that all were staunch defenders of the cause of freedom have been passed over. The military experience gathered in Africa during the Congo civil wars, which may have been crucial to the slave revolution, is a non-issue in Haiti.[42] Not just because few Haitians are intimate with African history, but because Haitian historians (like everyone else) long assumed that victorious strategies could only come from the Europeans or the most Europeanized slaves. Words like Congo and Bossale carry negative connotations in the Caribbean today. Never mind that Haiti was born with a majority of Bossales. As the Auguste brothers have recently noted, no one wondered how the label "Congo" came to describe a purported political minority at a time when the bulk of the population was certainly African-born and probably from the Congo region.[43]

Jean-Baptiste Sans Souci is the Congo par excellence. He was the most renowned of the African rebels and the most effective from the point of view of both French and "colonial" higher ranks. He is a ghost that most Haitian historians—urban, literate, French speakers, as they all are—would rather lay to rest. "Mulatto" historian Beaubrun Ardouin, who helped launch Haitian historiography on a modern path, and whose thousands of pages have been pruned, acclaimed, plagiarized, and contested, is known for his hatred of Christophe and his harsh criticism of the dark-skinned heroes of Haitian independence. Yet, when it came to Sans Souci, Ardouin the "mulatto" took the black Creole's side. Describing a meeting during the negotiations over the leadership in which a "courageous," "energetic," "distinguished," "intelligent" and (suddenly) "good-looking" Christophe used his legendary magnetism to influence Sans Souci, Ardouin writes:

> [B]randishing his sword, (Christophe) moved toward (Sans Souci) and asked him to declare whether or not he did not acknowledge him as a général, his superior. . . . [S]ubjugated by the ascendance of a civilized man, and a former commander at that, the African told him: "General, what do you want to do?" "You are calling me général (replied Christophe); then, you do acknowledge me as your chief, since you are not a general yourself." Sans Souci did not dare reply. . . . The Barbarian was defeated.[44]

Ardouin is quick to choose sides not only because he may feel culturally closer to Christophe, a "civilized man," but also because, as a nationalist historian, he needs Christophe against Sans Souci.

As the first independent modern state of the so-called Third World, Haiti experienced early all the trials of postcolonial nation-building. In contrast to the United States, the only postcolonial case before 1804, it did so within a context characterized by a dependent economy and freedom for all. Thus, while the elites' claims to state control required, as elsewhere, the partial appropriation of the culture-history of the masses, they also required, perhaps more than elsewhere, the silencing of dissent. Both the silencing of dissent and the building of state institutions started with the Louverture regime whose closest equivalent in post-independent Haiti was Henry I's kingdom. In short, Christophe's fame as a builder, both figuratively and literally, and his reputation as a ruthless leader are two sides of the same coin. Ardouin, a political kingmaker in his own time, knows this. Both he and Christophe belong to the same elites that must control and normalize the aspirations of the barbarians.[45]

Ardouin also needs Christophe against the French. In spite of the attributes that Ardouin abhors and that he finds elsewhere hard to reconcile with civilization, Christophe is part of the glory that Ardouin claims to be his past. Christophe beat the French; Sans Souci did not. Christophe erected these monuments to the honor of the black race, whereas Sans Souci, the African, nearly stalled the epic.

For Ardouin, as for many other Haitians, Sans Souci is an inconvenience inasmuch as the war within the war may prove to be a distraction from the main event of 1791–1804: the successful revolution that their ancestors launched against both slavery and colonialism and that the white world did its best to forget. Here, the silencing of Sans Souci the man and that of Sans Souci–Potsdam converge. They are silences of resistance, silences thrown against a superior silence, that which Western historiography has produced around the revolution of Saint-Domingue/Haiti. In the context of this silencing, which we explore in the next chapter, Potsdam remains a vague suggestion, the Colonel's death is a mere matter of fact, while the crumbling walls of Milot still stand as a last defense against oblivion.

An Unthinkable History

The Haitian Revolution as a Non-event

 3

The young woman stood up in the middle of my lecture. "Mr. Trouillot, you make us read all those white scholars. What can they know about slavery? Where were they when we were jumping off the boats? When we chose death over misery and killed our own children to spare them from a life of rape?"

I was scared and she was wrong. She was not reading white authors only and she never jumped from a slave ship. I was dumbfounded and she was angry; but how does one reason with anger? I was on my way to a Ph.D., and my teaching this course was barely a stopover, a way of paying the dues of guilt in this lily-white institution. She had taken my class as a mental break on her way to med school, or Harvard law, or some lily-white corporation.

I had entitled the course "The Black Experience in the Americas." I should have known better: it attracted the few black students around—plus a few courageous whites—and they were all expecting too much, much more than I could deliver. They wanted a life that no narrative could provide, even the best fiction. They wanted a life that only they could build right now, right here in the United States—except that they did not know this: they were too close to the unfolding story. Yet already I could see in their eyes that part of my lesson registered. I wanted them to know that slavery did not happen only in Georgia and Mississippi. I wanted them to learn that the African connection was more complex and tortuous than they had ever imagined, that the U.S. monopoly on both blackness and racism was itself a racist plot. And she had broken the spell on her way to Harvard law. I was a novice and so was she, each of us struggling with the history we chose, each of us also fighting an imposed oblivion.

Ten years later, I was visiting another institution with a less prestigious clientele and more modest dreams when another young black woman, the same age but much more timid, caught me again by surprise. "I am tired," she said, "to hear about this slavery stuff. Can we hear the story of the black millionaires?" Had times changed so fast, or were their different takes on slavery reflections of class differences?

I flashed back to the first woman clinging so tightly to that slave boat. I understood better why she wanted to jump, even once, on her way to Harvard law, med school, or wherever. Custodian of the future for an imprisoned race whose young males do not live long enough to have a past, she needed this narrative of resistance. Nietzsche was wrong: this was no extra baggage, but a necessity for the journey, and who was I to say that it was no better a past than a bunch of fake millionaires, or a medal of St. Henry and the crumbling walls of a decrepit palace?

I wish I could shuffle the years and put both young women in the same room. We would have shared stories not yet in the archives. We would have read Ntozake Shange's tale of a colored girl dreaming of Toussaint Louverture and the revolution that the world forgot. Then we would have returned to the planters' journals, to econometric history and its industry of statistics, and none of us would be afraid of the numbers. Hard facts are no more frightening than darkness. You can play with them if you are with friends. They are scary only if you read them alone.

We all need histories that no history book can tell, but they are not in the classroom—not the history classrooms, anyway. They are in the lessons we learn at home, in poetry and childhood games, in what is left of history when we close the history books with their verifiable facts. Otherwise, why would a black woman born and raised in the richest country of the late twentieth century be more afraid to talk about slavery than a white planter in colonial Saint-Domingue just days before rebellious slaves knocked on his door?

This is a story for young black Americans who are still afraid of the dark. Although they are not alone, it may tell them why they feel they are.

Unthinking a Chimera

In 1790, just a few months before the beginning of the insurrection that shook Saint-Domingue and brought about the revolutionary birth of independent Haiti, French colonist La Barre reassured his metropolitan wife of the peaceful state of life in the tropics. He wrote: "There is no movement among our Negroes. . . . They don't even think of it. They are very tranquil and obedient. A revolt among them is impossible." And again: "We have nothing to fear on the part of the Negroes; they are tranquil and obedient." And again: "The Negroes are very obedient and always will be. We sleep with doors and windows wide open. Freedom for Negroes is a chimera."[1]

Historian Roger Dorsinville, who cites these words, notes that a few months later the most important slave insurrection in recorded history had reduced to insignificance such abstract arguments about Negro obedience. I am not so sure. When reality does not coincide with deeply held beliefs, human beings tend to phrase interpretations that force reality within the scope of these beliefs. They devise formulas to repress the unthinkable and to bring it back within the realm of accepted discourse.

La Barre's views were by no means unique. Witness this manager who constantly reassured his patrons in almost similar words: "I live tranquilly in the midst of them without a single thought of their uprising unless that was fomented by the whites themselves."[2] There were doubts at times. But the planters' practical precautions aimed at stemming individual actions or, at worst, a sudden riot. No one in Saint-Domingue or elsewhere worked out a plan of response to a general insurrection.

Indeed, the contention that enslaved Africans and their descendants could not envision freedom—let alone formulate strategies for gaining and securing such freedom—was based not so much on empirical evidence as on an ontology, an implicit organization of the world and its inhabitants. Although by no means monolithic, this worldview was widely shared by whites in Europe and the Americas and by many non-white plantation owners as well. Although it left room for variations, none of these variations included the possibility of a revolutionary uprising in the slave plantations, let alone a successful one leading to the creation of an independent state.

The Haitian Revolution thus entered history with the peculiar characteristic of being unthinkable even as it happened. Official debates and publications of the times, including the long list of pamphlets on Saint-Domingue published in France from 1790 to 1804, reveal the incapacity of most contemporaries to understand the ongoing revolution on its own terms.[3] They could read the news only with their ready-made categories, and these categories were incompatible with the idea of a slave revolution.

The discursive context within which news from Saint-Domingue was discussed as it happened has important consequences for the historiography of Saint-Domingue/Haiti. If some events cannot be accepted even as they occur, how can they be assessed later? In other words, can historical narratives convey plots that are unthinkable in the world within which these narratives take place? How does one write a history of the impossible?

The key issue is not ideological. Ideological treatments are now more current in Haiti itself (in the epic or bluntly political interpretations of the revolution favored by some Haitian writers) than in the more rigorous handling of the evidence by professionals in Europe or in North America. The international scholarship on the Haitian Revolution has been rather sound by modern standards of evidence since at least the 1940s. The issue is rather epistemological and, by inference, methodological in the broadest sense. Standards of evidence notwithstanding, to what extent has modern historiography of the Haitian Revolution—as part of a continuous Western discourse on slavery, race, and colonization—broken the iron bonds of the philosophical milieu in which it was born?

A Certain Idea of Man

The West was created somewhere at the beginning of the sixteenth century in the midst of a global wave of material and symbolic transformations. The definitive expulsion of the Muslims from Europe, the so-called voyages of exploration, the first developments of merchant colonialism, and the maturation of the absolutist state set the stage for the rulers and merchants of Western Christendom to conquer Europe and the rest of the world. This historical itinerary was political, as evidenced by the now well-known names that it evokes—Columbus, Magellan, Charles V, the Hapsburgs, and the turning moments that set its pace—the reconquest of Castile and of Aragon, the laws of Burgos, the transmission of papal power from the Borgias to the Medicis.

These political developments paralleled the emergence of a new symbolic order. The invention of the Americas (with Waldseemuller, Vespucci, and Balboa), the simultaneous invention of Europe, the division of the Mediterranean by an imaginary line going from the south of Cadiz to the north of Constantinople, the westernization of Christianity, and the invention of a Greco-Roman past to Western Europe were all part of the process through which Europe became the West.[4] What we call the Renaissance, much more an invention in its own right than a rebirth, ushered in a number of philosophical questions to which politicians, theologians, artists, and soldiers provided both concrete and abstract answers. What is Beauty? What is Order? What is the State? But also and above all: What is Man?

Philosophers who discussed that last issue could not escape the fact that colonization was going on as they spoke. Men (Europeans) were conquering, killing, dominating, and enslaving other beings thought to be equally human, if only by some. The contest between Bartolomé de Las Casas and Juan Ginés de Sepúlveda at Valladolid on the nature and fate of the Indians in 1550–1551 was only one instance of this continuous encounter between the symbolic and the practical. Whence, the very ambiguities of the early Las Casas who believed both in colonization and in the humanity of the Indians and found it impossible to reconcile the two. But despite Las Casas and others, the Renaissance did not—could not—settle the question of the ontological nature of conquered peoples. As we well know, Las Casas himself offered a poor and ambiguous compromise that he was to regret later: freedom for the savages (the Indians), slavery for the barbarians (the Africans). Colonization won the day.

The seventeenth century saw the increased involvement of England, France, and the Netherlands in the Americas and in the slave trade. The eighteenth century followed the same path with a touch of perversity: the more European merchants and mercenaries bought and conquered other men and women, the more European philosophers wrote and talked about Man. Viewed from outside the West, with its extraordinary increase in both philosophical musings and concrete attention to colonial practice, the century of the Enlightenment was also a century of confusion. There is no single view of blacks—or of any non-white group, for that matter—even within discrete European populations. Rather, non-European groups were forced to enter into various philosophical, ideological, and practical schemes. Most important for our purposes is that all these schemes recognized degrees of humanity. Whether these connecting ladders ranked chunks of humanity on ontological, ethical, political, scientific, cultural, or simply pragmatic grounds, the fact is that all assumed and reasserted that, ultimately, some humans were more so than others.

For indeed, in the horizon of the West at the end of the century, Man (with a capital M) was primarily European and male. On this single point everyone who mattered agreed. Men were also, to a lesser degree, females of European origins, like the French "citoyennes," or ambiguous whites, such as European Jews. Further down were peoples tied to strong state structures: Chinese, Persians, Egyptians, who exerted a different fascination on some Europeans for being at the same time more "advanced" and yet potentially more evil than other Westerners. On reflection, and only for a timid minority, Man could also be westernized man, the complacent colonized. The benefit of doubt did not extend very far: westernized (or more properly, "westernizable") humans, natives of Africa or of the Americas, were at the lowest level of this nomenclature.[5]

Negative connotations linked to skin colors increasingly regrouped as "black" had first spread in Christendom in the late Middle Ages. They were reinforced by the fanciful descriptions of medieval geographers and travellers. Thus, the word "nègre" entered French dictionaries and glossaries with negative undertones increasingly precise from its first appearances in the 1670s to the universal dictionaries that augured the Encyclopedia.[6] By the middle of the eighteenth century, "black" was almost universally bad. What had happened in the meantime, was the expansion of African-American slavery.

Indeed, the rather abstract nomenclature inherited from the Renaissance was altogether reproduced, reinforced, and challenged by colonial practice and the philosophical literature. That is, eighteenth-century colonial practice brought to the fore both the certitudes and the ambiguities of the ontological order that paralleled the rise of the West.

Colonization provided the most potent impetus for the transformation of European ethnocentrism into scientific racism. In the early 1700s, the ideological rationalization of Afro-American slavery relied increasingly on explicit formulations of the ontological order inherited from the Renaissance. But in so doing, it also transformed the Renaissance worldview by bringing its purported inequalities much closer to the very practices that confirmed them. Blacks were inferior and therefore enslaved; black slaves behaved badly and were therefore inferior. In short, the practice of slavery in the Americas secured the blacks' position at the bottom of the human world.

With the place of blacks now guaranteed at the bottom of the Western nomenclature, anti-black racism soon became the central element of planter ideology in the Caribbean. By the middle of the eighteenth century, the arguments justifying slavery in the Antilles and North America relocated in Europe where they blended with the racist strain inherent in eighteenth-century rationalist thought. The literature in French is telling, though by no means unique. Buffon fervently supported a monogenist viewpoint: blacks were not, in his view, of a different species. Still, they were different enough to be destined to slavery. Voltaire disagreed, but only in part. Negroes belonged to a different species, one culturally destined to be slaves. That the material well-being of many of these thinkers was often indirectly and, sometimes, quite directly linked to the exploitation of African slave labor may not have been irrelevant to their learned opinions. By the time of the American Revolution, scientific racism, whose rise many historians wrongly attribute to the nineteenth century, was already a feature of the ideological landscape of the Enlightenment on both sides of the Atlantic.[7]

Thus the Enlightenment exacerbated the fundamental ambiguity that dominated the encounter between ontological discourse and colonial practice. If the philosophers did reformulate some of the answers inherited from the Renaissance, the question "What is Man?" kept stumbling against the practices of domination and of merchant accumulation. The gap between abstraction and practice grew or, better said, the handling of the contradictions between the two became much more sophisticated, in part because philosophy provided as many answers as colonial practice itself. The Age of the Enlightenment was an age in which the slave drivers of Nantes bought titles of nobility to better parade with philosophers, an age in which a freedom fighter such as Thomas Jefferson owned slaves without bursting under the weight of his intellectual and moral contradictions.

In the name of freedom and democracy also, in July 1789, just a few days before the storming of the Bastille, a few planters from Saint-Domingue met in Paris to petition the newly formed French Assembly to accept in its midst twenty representatives from the Caribbean. The planters had derived this number from the population of the islands, using roughly the mathematics used in France to proportion metropolitan representatives in the Assembly. But they had quite advertently counted the black slaves and the *gens de couleur* as part of the population of the islands whereas, of course, they were claiming no rights of suffrage for these non-whites. Honoré Gabriel Riquetti, Count of Mirabeau, took the stand to denounce the planters' skewed mathematics. Mirabeau told the Assembly:

> Are the colonies placing their Negroes and their *gens de couleur* in the class of men or in that of the beasts of burden?
>
> If the Colonists want the Negroes and *gens de couleur* to count as men, let them enfranchise the first; that all may be electors, that all may be elected. If not, we beg them to observe that in proportioning the number of deputies to the population of France, we have taken into consideration neither the number of our horses nor that of our mules.[8]

Mirabeau wanted the French Assembly to reconcile the philosophical positions explicit in the Declaration of Rights of Man and its political stance on the colonies. But the declaration spoke of "the Rights of Man and Citizen," a title which denotes, as Tzvetan Todorov reminds us, the germ of a contradiction.[9] In this case the citizen won over the man—at least over the non-white man. The National Assembly granted only six deputies to the sugar colonies of the Caribbean, a few more than they deserved if only the whites had been counted but many less than if the Assembly had recognized the full political rights of the blacks and the *gens de couleur.* In the mathematics of realpolitik, the half-million slaves of Saint Domingue-Haiti and the few hundred thousands of the other colonies were apparently worth three deputies—white ones at that.

The ease with which the Assembly bypassed its own contradictions, an echo of the mechanisms by which black slaves came to account for three-fifths of a person in the United States, permeated the practices of the Enlightenment. Jacques Thibau doubts that contemporaries found a dichotomy between the France of the slavers and that of the philosophers. "Was not the Western, maritime France, an integral part of France of the Enlightenment?"[10] Louis Sala-Molins further suggests that we distinguish between the advocacy of slavery and the racism of the time: one could oppose the first (on practical grounds) and not the other (on philosophical ones). Voltaire, notably, was racist, but often opposed slavery on practical rather than moral grounds. So did David Hume, not because he believed in the equality of blacks, but because, like Adam Smith, he considered the whole business too expensive. Indeed, in France as in England, the arguments for or against slavery in formal political arenas were more often than not couched in pragmatic terms, notwithstanding the mass appeal of British abolitionism and its religious connotations.

The Enlightenment, nevertheless, brought a change of perspective. The idea of progress, now confirmed, suggested that men were perfectible. Therefore, subhumans could be, theoretically at least, perfectible. More important, the slave trade was running its course, and the economics of slavery would be questioned increasingly as the century neared its end. Perfectibility became an argument in the practical debate: the westernized other looked increasingly more profitable to the West, especially if he could become a free laborer. A French memoir of 1790 summarized the issue: "It is perhaps not impossible to civilize the Negro, to bring him to principles and *make a man out of him*: there would be more to gain than to buy and sell him." Finally, we should not underestimate the loud anti-colonialist stance of a small, elitist but vocal group of philosophers and politicians.[11]

The reservations expressed in the metropolis had little impact within the Caribbean or in Africa. Indeed, the slave trade increased in the years 1789–1791 while French politicians and philosophers were debating more vehemently than ever on the rights of humanity. Further, few politicians or philosophers attacked racism, colonialism, and slavery in a single blow and with equal vehemence. In France as in England colonialism, pro-slavery rhetoric, and racism intermingled and supported one another without ever becoming totally confused. So did their opposites. That allowed much room for multiple positions.[12]

Such multiplicity notwithstanding, there was no doubt about Western superiority, only about its proper use and effect. *L'Histoire des deux Indes*, signed by Abbé Raynal with philosopher and encyclopedist Denis Diderot acting as ghost—and, some would say, premier—contributor to the anti-colonialist passages, was perhaps the most radical critique of colonialism from the France of the Enlightenment.[13] Yet the book never fully questioned the ontological principles behind the colonialist enterprise, namely that the differences between forms of humanity were not only of degree but of kind, not historical but primordial. The polyphony of the book further limited its anti-slavery impact.[14] Bonnet rightly points that the *Histoire* is a book that reveres at once the immobile vision of the noble savage and the benefits of industry and human activity.[15]

Behind the radicalism of Diderot and Raynal stood, ultimately, a project of colonial management. It did indeed include the abolition of slavery, but only in the long term, and as part of a process that aimed at the better control of the colonies.[16] Access to human status did not lead *ipso facto* to self-determination. In short, here again, as in Condorcet, as in Mirabeau, as in Jefferson, when all is said and done, there are degrees of humanity.

The vocabulary of the times reveals that gradation. When one talked of the biological product of black and of white intercourse, one spoke of "man of color" as if the two terms do not necessarily go together: unmarked humanity is white. The captain of a slave boat bluntly emphasized this implicit opposition between white "Men" and the rest of humankind. After French supporters of the free coloreds in Paris created the *Société des Amis des Noirs*, the pro-slavery captain proudly labelled himself "l'Ami des Hommes." The Friends of the Blacks were not necessarily Friends of Man.[17] The lexical opposition Man-versus-Native (or Man-versus-Negro) tinted the European literature on the Americas from 1492 to the Haitian Revolution and beyond. Even the radical duo Diderot-Raynal did not escape it. Recounting an early Spanish exploration, they write: "Was not this handful of *men* surrounded by an innumerable multitude of *natives* . . . seized with alarm and terror, well or ill founded?"[18]

One will not castigate long-dead writers for using the words of their time or for not sharing ideological views that we now take for granted. Lest accusations of political correctness trivialize the issue, let me emphasize that I am not suggesting that eighteenth-century men and women *should* have thought about the fundamental equality of humankind in the same way some of us do today. On the contrary, I am arguing that they *could not* have done so. But I am also drawing a lesson from the understanding of this historical impossibility. The Haitian Revolution did challenge the ontological and political assumptions of the most radical writers of the Enlightenment. *The events that shook up Saint-Domingue from 1791 to 1804 constituted a sequence for which not even the extreme political left in France or in England had a conceptual frame of reference.* They were "unthinkable" facts in the framework of Western thought.

Pierre Bourdieu defines the unthinkable as that for which one has no adequate instruments to conceptualize. He writes: "In the unthinkable of an epoch, there is all that one cannot think for want of ethical or political inclinations that predispose to take it in account or in consideration, but also that which one cannot think for want of instruments of thought such as problematics, concepts, methods, techniques."[19] The unthinkable is that which one cannot conceive within the range of possible alternatives, that which perverts all answers because it defies the terms under which the questions were phrased. In that sense, the Haitian Revolution was unthinkable in its time: it challenged the very framework within which proponents and opponents had examined race, colonialism, and slavery in the Americas.

Prelude to the News: The Failure of Categories

Between the first slave shipments of the early 1500s and the 1791 insurrection of northern Saint-Domingue, most Western observers had treated manifestations of slave resistance and defiance with the ambivalence characteristic of their overall treatment of colonization and slavery. On the one hand, resistance and defiance did not exist, since to acknowledge them was to acknowledge the humanity of the enslaved.[20] On the other hand, since resistance occurred, it was dealt with quite severely, within or around the plantations. Thus, next to a discourse that claimed the contentment of slaves, a plethora of laws, advice, and measures, both legal and illegal, were set up to curb the very resistance denied in theory.

Publications by and for planters, as well as plantation journals and correspondence, often mixed both attitudes. Close as some were to the real world, planters and managers could not fully deny resistance, but they tried to provide reassuring certitudes by trivializing all its manifestations. Resistance did not exist as a global phenomenon. Rather, each case of unmistakable defiance, each possible instance of resistance was treated separately and drained of its political content. Slave A ran away because he was particularly mistreated by his master. Slave B was missing because he was not properly fed. Slave X killed herself in a fatal tantrum. Slave Y poisoned her mistress because she was jealous. The runaway emerges from this literature—which still has its disciples—as an animal driven by biological constraints, at best as a pathological case. The rebellious slave in turn is a maladjusted Negro, a mutinous adolescent who eats dirt until he dies, an infanticidal mother, a deviant. To the extent that sins of humanity are acknowledged they are acknowledged only as evidence of a pathology.

In retrospect, this argument is not very convincing to anyone aware of the infinite spectrum of human reactions to forms of domination. It is at best an anemic caricature of methodological individualism. Would each single explanation be true, the sum of all of them would say little of the causes and effects of the repetition of such cases.

In fact, this argument didn't convince the planters themselves. They held on to it because it was the only scheme that allowed them not to deal with the issue as a mass phenomenon. That latter interpretation was inconceivable. Built into any system of domination is the tendency to proclaim its own normalcy. To acknowledge resistance as a mass phenomenon is to acknowledge the possibility that something is wrong with the system. Caribbean planters, much as their counterparts in Brazil and in the United States, systematically rejected that ideological concession, and their arguments in defense of slavery were central to the development of scientific racism.

Yet, as time went on, the succession of plantation revolts, and especially the consolidation—in Jamaica, and in the Guianas—of large colonies of runaways with whom colonial governments had to negotiate, gradually undermined the image of submission and the complementary argument of pathological misadaptation. However much some observers wanted to see in these massive departures a sign of the force that nature exerted on the animal-slave, the possibility of mass resistance penetrated Western discourse.

The penetration was nevertheless circumspect. When Louis-Sébastien Mercier announced an avenger of the New World in 1771, it was in a novel of anticipation, a utopia.[21] The goal was to warn Europeans of the fatalities that awaited them if they did not change their ways. Similarly, when the duo Raynal-

Diderot spoke of a black Spartacus, it was not a clear prediction of a Louverture-type character, as some would want with hindsight.[22] In the pages of the *Histoire des deux Indes* where the passage appears, the threat of a black Spartacus is couched as a warning. The reference is not to Saint-Domingue but to Jamaica and to Guyana where "there are two established colonies of fugitive negroes. . . . These flashes of lightning announce the thunder, and the negroes lack only a chief courageous enough to drive them to *revenge and to carnage*. Where is he, this great man whom nature owes *perhaps* to the honor of the human species? Where is this new Spartacus? . . ."[23]

In this version of the famous passage, modified in successive editions of the *Histoire*, the most radical stance is in the unmistakable reference to a single human species. But just as with Las Casas, just as with Buffon or the left of the French Assembly, the practical conclusions from what looks like a revolutionary philosophy are ambiguous. In Diderot-Raynal, as in the few other times it appears in writing, the evocation of a slave rebellion was primarily a rhetorical device. The concrete possibility of such a rebellion flourishing into a revolution and a modern black state was still part of the unthinkable.

Indeed, the political appeal—if appeal there was—is murky. To start with, Diderot's interlocutors are not the enslaved masses nor even the Spartacus who may or may not rise in an uncertain future. Diderot here is the voice of the enlightened West admonishing its colonialist counterpart.[24]

Second and more important, "slavery" was at that time an easy metaphor, accessible to a large public who knew that the word stood for a number of evils except perhaps the evil of itself. Slavery in the parlance of the philosophers could be whatever was wrong with European rule in Europe and elsewhere. To wit, the same Diderot applauded U.S. revolutionaries for having "burned their chains," for having "refused slavery." Never mind that some of them owned slaves. The *Marseillaise* was also a cry against "slavery."[25] Mulatto *slave owners* from the Caribbean told the French Assembly that their status as second-class free men was equivalent to slavery.[26] This metaphorical usage permeated the discourse of various nascent disciplines from philosophy to political economy up to Marx and beyond. References to slave resistance must thus be regarded in light of these rhetorical clichés. For if today we can read the successive "Declarations of the Rights of Man" or the U.S. Bill of Rights as naturally including every single human being, it is far from certain that this revisionist reading was the favored interpretation of the "men" of 1789 and 1791.[27]

Third, here as in the rarer texts that speak clearly of the right to insurrection, the possibility of a successful rebellion by slaves or colonized peoples is in a very distant future, still a specter of what might happen if the system remains unchanged.[28] The implication is, of course, that improvement within the system, or at any rate, starting from the system, could prevent carnage, surely not the philosophers' favorite outcome.

Fourth and finally, this was an age of change and inconsistency. Few thinkers had the politics of their philosophy. Radical action on the issue of slavery often came from unsuspected corners, notably in England or in the United States.[29] After examining the contradictions of the *Histoire*, Michèle Duchet concludes that the book is politically reformist and philosophically revolutionary. But even the philosophical revolution is not as neat as it first appears, and Duchet admits elsewhere that for Raynal to civilize is to colonize.[30]

Contradictions were plentiful, within philosophy, within politics, and between the two, even within the radical left. They are clearly displayed in the tactics of the pro-mulatto lobby, the Société des Amis des Noirs. The Société's philosophical point of departure was, of course, the full equality of humankind: some of its founding members participated in drafting the Declaration of Rights of Man. But here again were degrees of humanity. The sole sustained campaign of the self-proclaimed Friends of the Blacks was their effort to guarantee the civil and political rights of free mulatto owners. This emphasis was not simply a tactical maneuver. Many members on the left side of the Assembly went way beyond the call of duty to emphasize that not all blacks were equally worth defending. On December 11, 1791, Grégoire, for instance, denounced the danger of suggesting political rights for black slaves. "To give political rights to men who do not know their duties would be perhaps like placing a sword in the hands of a madman."[31]

Contradictions were no less obvious elsewhere. Under a pseudonym evoking both Judaity and blackness, Condorcet demonstrated all the evils of slavery but then called for *gradual* abolition.[32] Abolitionist Diderot hailed the American Revolution that had retained slavery. Jean-Pierre Brissot asked his friend Jefferson, whose stance on slavery was not questioned in France, to join the Ami des Noirs![33] Marat and—to a much lesser extent—Robespierre aside, few leading French revolutionaries recognized the right of white Frenchmen to revolt against colonialism, the same right whose application they admired in British North America.

To sum up, in spite of the philosophical debates, in spite of the rise of abolitionism, the Haitian Revolution was unthinkable in the West not only because it challenged slavery and racism but because of the way it did so. When the insurrection first broke in northern Saint-Domingue, a number of radical writers in Europe and very few in the Americas had been willing to acknowledge, with varying reservations—both practical and philosophical—the humanity of the enslaved. Almost none drew from this acknowledgment the necessity to abolish slavery immediately. Similarly, a handful of writers had evoked intermittently and, most often, metaphorically the possibility of mass resistance among the slaves. Almost none had actually conceded that the slaves could—let alone should—indeed revolt.[34] Louis Sala-Molins claims that slavery was the ultimate test of the Enlightenment. We can go one step further: The Haitian Revolution was the ultimate test to the universalist pretensions of both the French and the American revolutions. And they both failed. *In 1791, there is no public debate on the record, in France, in England, or in the United States on the right of black slaves to achieve self-determination, and the right to do so by way of armed resistance.*

Not only was the Revolution unthinkable and, therefore, unannounced in the West, it was also—to a large extent—unspoken among the slaves themselves. By this I mean that the Revolution was not preceded or even accompanied by an explicit intellectual discourse.[35] One reason is that most slaves were illiterate and the printed word was not a realistic means of propaganda in the context of a slave colony. But another reason is that the claims of the revolution were indeed too radical to be formulated in advance of its deeds. Victorious practice could assert them only after the fact. In that sense, the revolution was indeed at the limits of the thinkable, even in Saint-Domingue, even among the slaves, even among its own leaders.

We need to recall that the key tenets of the political philosophy that became explicit in Saint-Domingue/Haiti between 1791 and 1804 were not accepted by world public opinion until after World War II. When the Haitian Revolution broke out, only five percent of a world population estimated at nearly 800 million would have been considered "free" by modern standards. The British campaign for abolition of the slave *trade* was in its infancy; the abolition of slavery was even further behind. Claims about the fundamental uniqueness of humankind, claims about the ethical irrelevance of racial categories or of geographical situation to matters of governance and, certainly, claims about the right of *all* peoples to self-determination went against received wisdom in the Atlantic world and beyond. Each could reveal itself in Saint-Domingue only through practice. By necessity, the Haitian Revolution thought itself out politically and philosophically as it was taking place. Its project, increasingly radicalized throughout thirteen years of combat, was revealed in successive spurts. Between and within its unforeseen stages, discourse always lagged behind practice.

The Haitian Revolution expressed itself mainly through its deeds, and it is through political practice that it challenged Western philosophy and colonialism. It did produce a few texts whose philosophical import is explicit, from Louverture's declaration of Camp Turel to the Haitian Act of Independence and the Constitution of 1805. But its intellectual and ideological newness appeared most clearly with each and every political threshold crossed, from the mass insurrection (1791) to the crumbling of the colonial apparatus (1793), from general liberty (1794) to the conquest of the state machinery (1797–98), from Louverture's taming of that machinery (1801) to the proclamation of Haitian independence with Dessalines (1804). Each and every one of these steps—leading up to and culminating in the emergence of a modern "black state," still largely part of the unthinkable until the twentieth century—challenged further the ontological order of the West and the global order of colonialism.

This also meant that the Haitian revolutionaries were not overly restricted by previous ideological limits set by professional intellectuals in the colony or elsewhere, that they could break new ground—and, indeed, they did so repeatedly. But it further meant that philosophical and political debate in the West, when it occurred, could only be reactive. It dealt with the impossible only after that impossible had become fact; and even then, the facts were not always accepted as such.

Battle in Saint-Domingue, a contemporary engraving

Dealing with the Unthinkable: The Failures of Narration

When the news of the massive uprising of August 1791 first hit France, the most common reaction among interested parties was disbelief: the facts were too unlikely; the news had to be false. Only the most vocal representatives of the planter party took them seriously, in part because they were the first to be informed via their British contacts, in part because they had the most to lose if indeed the news was verified. Others, including colored plantation owners then in France and most of the left wing of the French assembly, just could not reconcile their perception of blacks with the idea of a large-scale black rebellion.[36] In an impassioned speech delivered to the French assembly on 30 October 1791, delegate Jean-Pierre Brissot, a founding member of the *Amis des Noirs* and moderate anti-colonialist, outlined the reasons why the news had to be false: a) anyone who knew the blacks had to realize that it was simply impossible for fifty thousand of them to get together so fast and act in concert; b) slaves could not conceive of rebellion on their own, and mulattoes and whites were not so insane as to incite them to full-scale violence; c) even if the slaves had rebelled in such huge numbers, the superior French troops would have defeated them. Brissot went on:

> What are 50,000 men, badly armed, undisciplined and used to fear when faced with 1,800 Frenchmen used to fearlessness? What! In 1751, Dupleix and a few hundred Frenchmen could break the siege of Pondichéri and beat a well-equipped army of 100,000 Indians, and M. de Blanchelande with French troops and cannons would fear a much inferior troop of blacks barely armed?[37]

With such statements from a "Friend," the revolution did not need enemies. Yet so went majority opinion from left to center-right within the Assembly until the news was confirmed beyond doubt. Confirmation did not change the dominant views. When detailed news reached France, many observers were frightened not by the revolt itself but by the fact that the colonists had appealed to the English.[38] A serious long-term danger coming from the blacks was still unthinkable. Slowly though, the size of the uprising sank in. Yet even then, in France as in Saint-Domingue, as indeed in Jamaica, Cuba, and the United States before, planters, administrators, politicians, or ideologues found explanations that forced the rebellion back within their worldview, shoving the facts into the proper order of discourse. Since blacks could not have generated such a massive endeavor, the insurrection became an unfortunate repercussion of planters' miscalculations. It did not aim at revolutionary change, given its royalist influences. It was not supported by a majority of the slave population. It was due to outside agitators. It was the unforeseen consequence of various conspiracies connived by non-slaves. Every party chose its favorite enemy as the most likely conspirator behind the slave uprising. Royalist, British, mulatto, or Republican conspirators were seen or heard everywhere by dubious and interested witnesses. Conservative colonialists and anti-slavery republicans accused each other of being the brains behind the revolt. Inferences were drawn from writings that could not have possibly reached or moved the slaves of Saint-Domingue even if they knew how to read. In a revealing speech, deputy Blangilly urged his colleagues to consider the possibility that the rebellion was due, at least in part, to the slaves' natural desire for freedom—a possibility that most rejected then and later. Blangilly then proceeded to suggest what was in his view the most logical conclusion: a law for the amelioration of slavery.[39] Legitimate as it was, the slaves' natural desire for freedom could not be satisfied, lest it threaten France's interests.

For thirteen years at least, Western public opinion pursued this game of hide-and-seek with the news coming out of Saint-Domingue. With every new threshold, the discourse accommodated some of the irrefutable data, questioned others, and provided reassuring explanations for the new package so created. By the spring of 1792, for instance, even the most distant observer could no longer deny the extent of the rebellion, the extraordinary number of slaves and plantations involved, the magnitude of the colonists' material losses. But then, many even in Saint-Domingue argued that the disaster was temporary, that everything would return to order. Thus, an eyewitness commented: "If the whites and the free mulattoes knew what was good for them, and kept tightly together, it is quite possible that things would return to normal, *considering the ascendancy that the white has always had over the negroes.*"[40] Note the doubt (the witness is tempted to believe his eyes); but note also that the nomenclature has not moved. Worldview wins over the facts: white hegemony is natural and taken for granted; any alternative is still in the domain of the unthinkable. Yet this passage was written in December 1792. At that time, behind the political chaos and the many battles between various armed factions, Toussaint Louverture and his closest followers were building up the avant-garde that would push the revolution to the point of no return. Indeed, six months later, civil commissar Léger Félicité Sonthonax was forced to declare free all slaves willing to fight under the French republican flag. A few weeks after Sonthonax's proclamation, in August 1793, Toussaint Louverture raised the stakes with his proclamation from Camp Turel: immediate unconditional freedom and equality for all.

By then, the old conspiracy theories should have become irrelevant. Clearly, the Louverture party was not willing to take orders from colonists, French Jacobins, or agents of foreign powers. What was going on in Saint-Domingue was, by all definitions, the most important slave rebellion ever witnessed and it had developed its own dynamics. Surprisingly, conspiracy theories survived long enough to justify the trials of a few Frenchmen accused to have fomented or helped the rebellion, from Blanchelande, the old royalist governor of 1791, to republican governor Lavaux, to Félicité Sonthonax, the Jacobin.[41]

As the power of Louverture grew, every other party struggled to convince itself and its counterparts that the achievements of the black leadership would ultimately benefit someone else. The new black elite had to be, willingly or not, the pawn of a "major" international power. Or else, the colony would fall apart and a legitimate international state would pick up the pieces. Theories assuming chaos under black leadership continued even after Louverture and his closest lieutenants fully secured the military, political, and civil apparatus of the colony. If some foreign governments—notably the United States—were willing to maintain a guarded collaboration with the Louverture regime, it was in part because they "knew" that an independent state led by former slaves was an impossibility. Toussaint himself may have not believed in the possibility of independence whereas, for all practical purposes, he was ruling Saint-Domingue as if it were independent.

Opinion in Saint-Domingue, in North America, and in Europe constantly dragged after the facts. Predictions, when they were made, revealed themselves useless. Once the French expedition of reconquest was launched in 1802, pundits were easily convinced that France would win the war. In England, the *Cobbet Political Register* doubted that Toussaint would even oppose a resistance: he was likely to flee the country.[42] Leclerc himself, the commander of the French forces, predicted in early February that the war would be over in two weeks. He was wrong by two years, give or take two months. Yet planters in Saint-Domingue apparently shared his optimism. Leclerc reported to the Minister of the Marine that French residents were already enjoying the smell of victory. Newspapers in Europe and North and Latin America translated and commented on these dispatches: restoration was near.

By mid-1802, the debacle of Louverture's army seemed to verify that prophecy. The rejection of the truce by a significant minority of armed rebels—among whom was Sans Souci—and the full-scale resumption of military operations when the war within the war forced the colonial high brass to rejoin the revolution in the fall of 1802 did little to change the dominant views. Despite the alliance between the forces of Dessalines, Pétion, and Christophe and the repeated victories of the new revolutionary army, few outside of Saint-Domingue could foresee the outcome of this Negro rebellion. As late as the fall of 1803, a complete victory by the former slaves and the creation of an independent state was still unthinkable in Europe and North America. Only long after the 1804 declaration of independence would the fait accompli be ungraciously accepted.

Ungraciously, indeed. The international recognition of Haitian independence was even more difficult to gain than military victory over the forces of Napoleon. It took more time and more resources, more than a half century of diplomatic struggles. France imposed a heavy indemnity on the Haitian state in order to formally acknowledge its own defeat. The United States and the Vatican, notably, recognized Haitian independence only in the second half of the nineteenth century.

Diplomatic rejection was only one symptom of an underlying denial. The very deeds of the revolution were incompatible with major tenets of dominant Western ideologies. They remained so until at least the first quarter of this century. Between the Haitian independence and World War I, in spite of the successive abolitions of slavery, little changed within the various ladders that ranked humankind in the minds of the majorities in Europe and the Americas. In fact, some views deteriorated.[43] The nineteenth century was, in many respects, a century of retreat from some of the debates of the Enlightenment. Scientific racism, a growing but debated strain of Enlightenment thought, gained a much wider audience, further legitimizing the ontological nomenclature inherited from the Renaissance. The carving up of Asia and above all of Africa reinforced both colonial practice and ideology. Thus in most places outside of Haiti, more than a century after it happened, the revolution was still largely unthinkable history.

Erasure and Trivialization: Silences in World History

I have fleshed out two major points so far. First, the chain of events that constitute the Haitian Revolution was unthinkable before these events happened. Second, as they happened, the successive events within that chain were systematically recast by many participants and observers to fit a world of possibilities. That is, they were made to enter into narratives that made sense to a majority of Western observers and readers. I will now show how the revolution that was thought impossible by its contemporaries has also been silenced by historians. Amazing in this story is the extent to which historians have treated the events of Saint-Domingue in ways quite similar to the reactions of its Western contemporaries. That is, the narratives they build around these facts are strikingly similar to the narratives produced by individuals who thought that such a revolution was impossible.

The treatment of the Haitian Revolution in written history outside of Haiti reveals two families of tropes that are identical, in formal (rhetorical) terms, to figures of discourse of the late eighteenth century. The first kind of tropes are formulas that tend to erase directly the fact of a revolution. I call them, for short, formulas of erasure. The second kind tends to empty a number of singular events of their revolutionary content so that the entire string of facts, gnawed from all sides, becomes trivialized. I call them formulas of banalization. The first kind of tropes characterizes mainly the generalists and the popularizers—textbook authors, for example. The second are the favorite tropes of the specialists. The first type recalls the general silence on resistance in eighteenth-century Europe and North America. The second recalls the explanations of the specialists of the times, overseers and administrators in Saint-Domingue, or politicians in Paris. Both are formulas of silence.

The literature on slavery in the Americas and on the Holocaust suggests that there may be structural similarities in global silences or, at the very least, that erasure and banalization are not unique to the Haitian Revolution. At the level of generalities, some narratives cancel what happened through direct erasure of facts or their relevance. "It" did not *really* happen; it was not that bad, or that important. Frontal challenges to the fact of the Holocaust or to the relevance of Afro-American slavery belong to this type: The Germans did not really build gas chambers; slavery also happened to non-blacks. On a seemingly different plane, other narratives sweeten the horror or banalize the uniqueness of a situation by focusing on details: each convoy to Auschwitz can be explained on its own terms; some U.S. slaves were better fed than British workers; some Jews did survive. The joint effect of these two types of formulas is a powerful silencing: whatever has not been cancelled out in the generalities dies in the cumulative irrelevance of a heap of details. This is certainly the case for the Haitian Revolution.[44]

The general silence that Western historiography has produced around the Haitian Revolution originally stemmed from the incapacity to express the unthinkable, but it was ironically reinforced by the significance of the revolution for its contemporaries and for the generation immediately following. From 1791–1804 to the middle of the century, many Europeans and North Americans came to see that revolution as a litmus test for the black race, certainly for the capacities of all Afro-Americans. As Vastey's pronouncements on Sans Souci clearly show, Haitians did likewise.[45] Christophe's forts and palaces, the military efficiency of the former slaves, the impact of yellow fever on the French troops, and the relative weight of external factors on revolutionary dynamics figured highly in these debates. But if the revolution was significant for Haitians—and especially for the emerging Haitian elites as its self-proclaimed inheritors—to most foreigners it was primarily a lucky argument in a larger issue. Thus apologists and detractors alike, abolitionists and avowed racists, liberal intellectuals, economists, and slave owners used the events of Saint-Domingue to make their case, without regard to Haitian history as such. Haiti mattered to all of them, but only as pretext to talk about something else.[46]

With time, the silencing of the revolution was strengthened by the fate of Haiti itself. Ostracized for the better part of the nineteenth century, the country deteriorated both economically and politically—in part as a result of this ostracism.[47] As Haiti declined, the reality of the revolution seemed increasingly distant, an improbability which took place in an awkward past and for which no one had a rational explanation. The revolution that was unthinkable became a non-event.

Finally, the silencing of the Haitian Revolution also fit the relegation to an historical backburner of the three themes to which it was linked: racism, slavery, and colonialism. In spite of their importance in the formation of what we now call the West, in spite of sudden outbursts of interest as in the United States in the early 1970s, none of these themes has ever become a central concern of the historiographic tradition in a Western country. In fact, each of them, in turn, experienced repeated periods of silence of unequal duration and intensity in Spain, France, Britain, Portugal, The Netherlands, and the United States. The less colonialism and racism seem important in world history, the less important also the Haitian Revolution.

Thus not surprisingly, as Western historiographies remain heavily guided by national—if not always nationalist—interests, the silencing of Saint-Domingue/Haiti continues in historical writings otherwise considered as models of the genre. The silence is also reproduced in the textbooks and popular writings that are the prime sources on global history for the literate masses in Europe, in the Americas, and in large chunks of the Third World. This corpus has taught generations of readers that the period from 1776 to 1843 should properly be called "The Age of Revolutions." At the very same time, this corpus has remained silent on the most radical political revolution of that age.

In the United States, for example, with the notable exceptions of Henry Adams and W. E. B. Du Bois, few major writers conceded any significance to the Haitian Revolution in their historical writings up to the 1970s. Very few textbooks even mentioned it. When they did, they made of it a "revolt," a "rebellion." The ongoing silence of most Latin-American textbooks is still more tragic. Likewise, historians of Poland have paid little attention to the five thousand Poles involved in the Saint-Domingue campaigns. The silence also persists in England in spite of the fact that the British lost upward of sixty thousand men in eight years in an anti-French Caribbean campaign of which Saint-Domingue was the most coveted prize. The Haitian Revolution appears obliquely as part of *medical* history. The victor is disease, not the Haitians. The Penguin *Dictionary of Modern History*, a mass circulation pocket encyclopedia that covers the period from 1789 to 1945, has neither Saint-Domingue nor Haiti in its entries. Likewise, historian Eric Hobsbawm, one of the best analysts of this era, managed to write a book entitled *The Age of Revolutions, 1789–1843*, in which the Haitian Revolution scarcely appears. That Hobsbawm and the editors of the *Dictionary* would probably locate themselves quite differently within England's political spectrum is one indication that historical silences do not simply reproduce the overt political positions of the historians involved. What we are observing here is archival power at its strongest, the power to define what is and what is not a serious object of research and, therefore, of mention.[48]

The secondary role of conscious ideology and the power of the historical guild to decide relevance become obvious when we consider the case of France. France was the Western country most directly involved in the Haitian Revolution. France fought hard to keep Saint-Domingue and paid a heavy price for it. Napoleon lost nineteen French generals in Saint-Domingue, including his brother-in-law. France lost more men in Saint-Domingue than at Waterloo—as did England.[49] And although France recovered economically from the loss of Saint-Domingue, it had indeed surrendered the control of its most valuable colony to a black army and that loss had ended the dream of a French empire on the American mainland. The Haitian Revolution prompted the Louisiana Purchase. One would expect such "facts," none of which is controversial, to generate a chain of mentions, even if negative. Yet a perusal of French historical writings reveals multiple layers of silences.

The silencing starts with revolutionary France itself and is linked to a more general silencing of French colonialism. Although by the 1780s France was less involved than Britain in the slave trade, both slavery and colonialism were crucial to the French economy in the second half of the eighteenth century.[50] Historians debate only the extent—rather than the fact—of France's dependence on its Caribbean slave territories. All concur that Saint-Domingue was, at the time of its Revolution, the most valuable colony of the Western world and France's most important possession.[51] Many contemporaries would have agreed. Whenever the colonial issue was evoked, for instance in the assemblies, it was almost always mingled with Afro-American slavery and both were presented—most often, but not only, by the colonists—as a matter of vital importance for the future of France.[52]

Even if one leaves room, as one should, for rhetorical hyperbole, the fact that such rhetoric could be deployed is itself telling. But then, we discover a paradox. Every time the revolutionary assemblies, the polemists, journalists, and politicians that helped decide the fate of France between the outbreak of the French Revolution and the independence of Haiti evoked racism, slavery, and colonialism, they explicitly presented these issues as some of the most important questions that France faced, either on moral or on economic grounds. Yet the number of times they debated those same issues was strikingly limited. Considering both the weight of the colonies in French economic life and the heat of the rhetoric involved, the public debate was of short range. The number of individuals involved, the fact that most came from the elites, the limited amount of time that most participants devoted to these issues do not reflect the central place of colonialism in France's objective existence. They certainly do not reflect either the colonists' claim that the economic future of the country, or the *Amis des Noirs*' claim that the moral present of the nation was at stake. Recent research, including two important books by Yves Benot on colonialism and the French Revolution, has not challenged Daniel Resnick's earlier judgment that slavery was, even for France's libertarians, "a derivative concern."[53]

Still, revolutionary France left a trail of records on these subjects. Colonial management and both private and public communications between France and the Americas also left their paper trail. In short, the inaccessibility of sources is only relative. It cannot explain the massive disregard that French historiography shows for the colonial question and, by extension, for the Haitian Revolution. In fact, French historians continue to neglect the colonial question, slavery, resistance, and racism more than the revolutionary assemblies ever did. Most historians ignored or simply skipped whatever record there was. A few took the time for short and often derogatory passages on the Haitian revolutionaries before moving, as it were, to more important subjects.

The list of writers guilty of this silencing includes names attached to various eras, historical schools, and ideological positions, from Mme. de Staël, Alexis de Tocqueville, Adolphe Thiers, Alphonse de Lamartine, Jules Michelet, Albert Mathiez, and André Guérin, to Albert Soboul. Besides minor—and debatable—exceptions in the writings of Ernest Lavisse and, most especially Jean Jaurès, the silencing continues.[54] Larousse's glossy compilation of *The Great Events of World History*, meant to duplicate—and, one supposes, fashion—"the memory of humankind" produces a more polished silence than the Penguin pocket dictionary. It not only skips the Haitian Revolution; it attributes very little space to either slavery or colonialism.[55] Even the centennial celebrations of French slave emancipation in the 1948 did not stimulate a substantial literature on the subject. More surprising, neither the translation in French of C. L. R. James's *Black Jacobins* nor the publication of Aimé Césaire's *Toussaint Louverture*, which both place colonialism and the Haitian Revolution as a central question of the French Revolution, activated French scholarship.[56]

The public celebrations and the flood of publications that accompanied the Bicentennial of the French Revolution in 1989–1991 actively renewed the silence. Massive compilations of five hundred to a thousand pages on revolutionary France, published in the 1980s and directed by France's most prominent historians, show near total neglect both for colonial issues and the colonial revolution that forcibly brought them to the French estates. Sala-Molins describes and decries the near total erasure of Haiti, slavery, and colonization by French officials and the general public during ceremonies surrounding the Bicentennial.[57]

As this general silencing goes on, increased specialization within the historical guild leads to a second trend. Saint-Domingue/Haiti emerges at the intersection of various interests: colonial history, Caribbean or Afro-American history, the history of slavery, the history of New World peasantries. In any one of these subfields, it has now become impossible to silence the fact that a revolution took place. Indeed, the revolution itself, or even series of facts within it, have become legitimate topics for serious research within any of these subfields.

How interesting then, that many of the rhetorical figures used to interpret the mass of evidence accumulated by modern historians recall tropes honed by planters, politicians, and administrators both before and during the revolutionary struggle. Examples are plentiful, and I will only cite a few. Many analyses of marronage ("desertion" some still would say) come quite close to the biophysiological explanations preferred by plantation managers.[58] I have already sketched the pattern: slave A escaped because she was hungry, slave B because she was mistreated. . . . Similarly, conspiracy theories still provide many historians with a deus ex machina for the events of 1791 and beyond, just as in the rhetoric of the assemblymen of the times. The uprising must have been "prompted," "provoked," or "suggested" by some higher being than the slaves themselves: royalists, mulattoes, or other external agents.[59]

The search for external influences on the Haitian Revolution provides a fascinating example of archival power at work, not because such influences are impossible but because of the way the same historians treat contrary evidence that displays the internal dynamics of the revolution. Thus, many historians are more willing to accept the idea that slaves could have been influenced by whites or free mulattoes, with whom we know they had limited contacts, than they are willing to accept the idea that slaves could have convinced other slaves that they had the right to revolt. The existence of extended communication networks among slaves, of which we have only a glimpse, has not been a "serious" subject of historical research.[60]

Similarly, historians otherwise eager to find evidence of "external" participation in the 1791 uprising skip the unmistakable evidence that the rebellious slaves had their own program. In one of their earliest negotiations with representatives of the French government, the leaders of the rebellion did not ask for an abstractly couched "freedom." Rather, their most sweeping demands included three days a week to work on their own gardens and the elimination of the whip. These were not Jacobinist demands adapted to the tropics, nor royalist claims twice creolized. These were slave demands with the strong peasant touch that would characterize independent Haiti. But such evidence of an internal drive, although known to most historians, is not debated—not even to be rejected or interpreted otherwise. It is simply ignored, and this ignorance produces a silence of trivialization.

In that same vein, historian Robert Stein places most of the credit for the 1793 liberation of the slaves on Sonthonax. The commissar was a zealous Jacobin, a revolutionary in his own right, indeed perhaps the only white man to have evoked concretely and with sympathy the possibility of an armed insurrection among Caribbean slaves both *before the fact* and in a public forum.[61] We have no way to estimate the probable course of the Revolution without his invaluable contribution to the cause of freedom. But the point is not empirical. The point is that Stein's rhetoric echoes the very rhetoric first laid out in Sonthonax's trial. Implicit in that rhetoric is the assumption that the French connection is both sufficient and necessary to the Haitian Revolution. That assumption trivializes the slaves' independent sense of their right to freedom and the right to achieve this freedom by force of arms. Other writers tend to stay prudently away from the word "revolution," more often using such words as "insurgents," "rebels," "bands," and "insurrection." Behind this terminological fuzziness, these empirical blanks and these preferences in interpretation is the lingering impossibility, which goes back to the eighteenth century, of considering the former slaves as the main actors in the chain of events described.[62]

Yet since at least the first publication of C. L. R. James's classic, *The Black Jacobins* (but note the title), the demonstration has been well made to the guild that the Haitian Revolution is indeed a "revolution" in its own right by any definition of the word, and not an appendix of Bastille Day. But only with the popular reedition of James's book in 1962 and the civil rights movement in the United States did an international counter-discourse emerge, which fed on the historiography produced in Haiti since the nineteenth century. That counter-discourse was revitalized in the 1980s with the contributions of historians whose specialty was neither Haiti nor the Caribbean. Then, Eugene Genovese and—later—Robin Blackburn, echoing Henry Adams and W. E. B. Du Bois, insisted on the central role of the Haitian Revolution in the collapse of the entire system of slavery.[63] The impact of this counter-discourse remains limited, however, especially since Haitian researchers are increasingly distant from these international debates.

Thus, the historiography of the Haitian Revolution now finds itself marred by two unfortunate tendencies. On the one hand, most of the literature produced in Haiti remains respectful—too respectful, I would say—of the revolutionary leaders who led the masses of former slaves to freedom and independence. Since the early nineteenth century, the Haitian elites have chosen to respond to racist denigration with an epic discourse lauding *their* revolution. The epic of 1791–1804 nurtures among them a positive image of blackness quite useful in a white-dominated world. But the epic is equally useful on the home front. It is one of the rare historical alibis of these elites, an indispensable reference to their claims to power.

The empirical value of this epic tradition has steadily declined after its spectacular launching by such nineteenth-century giants as Thomas Madiou and Beaubrun Ardouin, and in spite of individual achievements of the early twentieth century. Unequal access to archives—products and symbols of neo-colonial domination—and the secondary role of empirical precision in this epic discourse continue to handicap Haitian researchers. They excel at putting facts into perspective, but their facts are weak, sometimes wrong, especially since the Duvalier regime explicitly politicized historical discourse.[64]

On the other hand, the history produced outside of Haiti is increasingly sophisticated and rich empirically. Yet its vocabulary and often its entire discursive framework recall frighteningly those of the eighteenth century. Papers and monographs take the tone of plantation records. Analyses of the revolution recall the letters of a La Barre, the pamphlets of French politicians, the messages of Leclerc to Bonaparte or, at best, the speech of Blangilly. I am quite willing to concede that the conscious political motives are not the same. Indeed again, that is part of my point. Effective silencing does not require a conspiracy, not even a political consensus. Its roots are structural. Beyond a stated—and most often sincere—political generosity, best described in U.S. parlance within a liberal continuum, the narrative structures of Western historiography have not broken with the ontological order of the Renaissance. This exercise of power is much more important than the alleged conservative or liberal adherence of the historians involved.

The solution may be for the two historiographic traditions—that of Haiti and that of the "foreign" specialists—to merge or to generate a new perspective that encompasses the best of each. There are indications of a move in this direction and some recent works suggest that it may become possible, sometime in the future, to write the history of the revolution that was, for long, unthinkable.[65]

But what I have said of the guild's reception of *The Black Jacobins*, of colonial history in France, and of slavery in U.S. history suggests also that neither a single great book nor even a substantial increase in slave resistance studies will fully uncover the silence that surrounds the Haitian Revolution. For the silencing of that revolution has less to do with Haiti or slavery than it has to do with the West.

Here again, what is at stake is the interplay between historicity 1 and historicity 2, between what happened and that which is said to have happened. What happened in Haiti between 1791 and 1804 contradicted much of what happened elsewhere in the world before and since. That fact itself is not surprising: the historical process is always messy, often enough contradictory. But what happened in Haiti also contradicted most of what the West has told both itself and others about itself. The world of the West basks in what François Furet calls the second illusion of truth: what happened is what must have happened. How many of us can think of any non-European population without the background of a global domination that now looks preordained? And how can Haiti, or slavery, or racism be more than distracting footnotes within that narrative order?

The silencing of the Haitian Revolution is only a chapter within a narrative of global domination. It is part of the history of the West and it is likely to persist, even in attenuated form, as long as the history of the West is not retold in ways that bring forward the perspective of the world. Unfortunately, we are not even close to such fundamental rewriting of world history, in spite of a few spectacular achievements.[66] The next chapter goes more directly, albeit from a quite unique angle, into this narrative of global domination which starts in Spain—or is it Portugal?—at the end of the fifteenth century.

Good Day, Columbus

 4

I walked past Vasco da Gama's body with premonitions of typhoons. I was in Portugal, at the Mosteiro dos Jéronimos, right where Europe started to redefine the world. Here Lisbon becomes Belém, in honor of Bethlehem, to absorb in the memory of the West the Orient where Christ was born. Here Da Gama knelt for his last blessing before facing the seven seas. Here he was brought back to be buried as if to engrave on this soil the history of uncharted oceans.

There were too many facts for that story to be simple—too many names crowding my thoughts, too many relics for a single image. This monastery was named after one Saint Jerome whose Hieronymite followers ran plantations in Santo Domingo. Its monstrance was made with gold that Da Gama, en route to Calicut, extorted from the Muslim sultan of Kilwa. Its main entrance faced an avenue called India. Everything here evoked an elsewhere and the hidden face of Europe: Christendom had not left a single continent untouched. The world started and ended here with a confusion of tongues and cultures.

The babel of Belém intruded on my memories: Jerome, Jéronimos, Hieronymites. Had not that name become a symbol of native resistance in the United States after an Indian born Goyahkla, in what used to be Mexico, was renamed Geronimo? My feelings as jumbled as the lands of Arizona, I kept wondering why so many Europeans deny that they created the United States. Didn't the line go straight from Afonso de Albuquerque to Albuquerque, New Mexico? Had not Da Gama died in Cochin less than five hundred years before Vietnam?

Outside the monastery, the sun over Belém spoke of pasts unknown and uncertain waters. I turned away from the Jéronimos. On the Avenue of Brazil, Lisbon flaunted further its long encounter with the seas. Yet the surfeit of names continued to defy the established story. There were too many signs here for history to remain official. Images of India, of Indians north, south, and west—from Calicut to Brazil, from Brazil to Arizona, persistent flavors of continents conquered in the name of spices and gold filled up the empty space between the monuments.

Moving among these ghosts, I savored the irony of this human landscape caught in the wheels of time. A clutter of colonial paraphernalia displayed itself on and off an avenue called Brazil—after the colony that for a brief moment was Portugal's metropolis. On my right, overlooking the Tagus, the Tower of Belém reminded me of piracy, of the time when Europe had to defend itself against its own. On my left, a few hundred yards from the Tower, the Monument to the Discoveries repackaged Portugal's past in a grandiose display of adventurous innocence.

A tribute to Prince Henry the Navigator, whose quincentennial it honored in 1960, the huge structure shows the Prince leading the Portuguese to the Discoveries. But the memorial was just too big to convince me of its chastity: its arched mass spoke of conquest, of Henry's desire to bend the onlooker under his will. Here Bethlehem met Brazil. Here Europe was confused about where it came from and where it had taken the world. Here anyone was at home and yet no one could rest in peace—not even Da Gama, whose remains were bought by the Portuguese in exchange for their weight in gold.

In the few square miles of Belém, the managers of history had tried repeatedly to impose a narrative. Perhaps they had tried too much. For in the monumental efforts of the Portuguese state to catch up with a history now eclipsed by nostalgia, I saw the nostalgia of the entire West for a history that it never lived, its constant longing for a place that exists only in its mind. The West was Calicut, Brazil, Cochin and Kilwa. The West was America, a dream of conquest and rapture. In the confusion of Belém, I could almost hear this line from Mon Oncle d'Amérique: "America does not exist. I know. I've been there."

Except that I was in Belém whence Europe's face looked no clearer than that of the Americas, no truer than that of Prince Henry, of whom there is no surviving picture. The Monument to the Discoveries had to invent a face for the Prince, just as Europe had to invent a face for the West. Belém's steady effort to patch up its own silences did not reflect on Portugal alone. It spoke of the entire West—of Spain, France, and the Netherlands, of Britain, Italy, and the United States—of all those who, like Columbus, had come from behind to displace Portugal in the reshaping of the world. And as much as I did not like it, as much as Prince Henry might disagree, it spoke also of me, of all the lands disturbed by their cacophony. Jerome, Jéronimos, Hieronymites—was anyone left untouched?

In 1549, soon after the Hieronymites started their plantations on Haitian soil, the Franciscans began their mission in Japan. I went back to my hotel, thinking of Columbus who once thought also that he had reached Japan. I could now glimpse the truth of my own history: The West does not exist. I know. I've been there.

October 12, 1492

History is messy for the people who must live it. For those within the shaky boundaries of Roman Christendom, the most important event of the year 1492 nearly happened in 1491. Late at night on November 25, 1491, Abu l-Qasim al-Muhli signed the treaties by which the Muslim kingdom of Granada surrendered to the Catholic kingdom of Castile, ending a war the issue of which had become clear a few months earlier. The transfer of power was scheduled for May, but some of the Muslim leaders decided not to wait for the Christian takeover and left town unexpectedly. Granada's Nasrid ruler, Muhammad XII Boabdil, rushed the capitulation. Thus, it was almost by accident that the flag of Castile and the cross of Christendom were raised over the tower of the Alhambra on January 2, 1492, rather than during the previous fall, as first expected, or the following spring, as scheduled.[1]

For actors and witnesses alike, the end of the *reconquista* was a disorderly series of occurrences, neither a single event, nor a single date. The end of the war and the signing of the treaties—both of which occurred in year 1491 of the Christian calendar—were as significant as the flight of the Muslim leaders, the raising of the Christian flag, or the glorious entry of the Catholic monarchs into the conquered city on January 6, 1492. The capitulation of Granada was, however, as close to a milestone as history in the making can get. Milestones are always set in regard to a past, and the past that Western Christendom had fashioned for itself projected the moving Spanish frontier as the southernmost rampart of the cross.

Since the Council of Clermont (1095), in part as an unexpected effect of three centuries of Islamic influence and control, Christian militants from both sides of the Pyrenees had heralded the reconquest of the Iberian peninsula as a sort of Christian *jihad*, the *via Hispania* to the Holy Land, a necessary stage on the road to the Holy Sepulchre. Popes, bishops, and kings had enlisted the limited—but highly symbolic—participation of Catholics from France to Scotland in various campaigns with such incentives as the partial remission of penance.

To be sure, cultural interpenetration between Christians, Moslems, and Jews went on in the peninsula and even north of the

Pyrenees long after Alfonso Henriques took Lisbon from the Arabs and placed Portugal under the tutelage of the church early in the twelfth century.[2] But the rhetoric of the popes and the merger of church and state power in the Iberian dominions, which went back to the Visigoths, created an ideological space where religions and cultures that mingled in daily life were seen as officially incompatible. Within that space, the defense of a Christendom, projected as pure and besieged, became a dominant idiom for the military campaigns.[3]

Both religious and military ardor declined in the second half of the fourteenth century, yet religion remained by default the closest thing to a "public arena" until the end of the Middle Ages, and religious figures the most able crowd leaders. Thus when religious and military enthusiasm, still intertwined, climbed together once more during Isabella's reign, the ultimate significance of the war for Christendom resurfaced unquestioned.[4] Even then, though, if many of those who lived the fall of Granada saw in it an occurrence of exceptional relevance, it was a milestone only for the peculiar individuals who paid attention to such things in the first place.

It mattered little then, in comparison, that a few months after entering Granada, the Catholic monarchs gave their blessing to a Genoese adventurer eager to reach India via a short-cut through the western seas.[5] It would matter little that the Genoese was wrong, having grossly underestimated the distance to be traveled. It probably mattered less, at the time, that the Genoese and his Castilian companions reached not the Indies but a tiny islet in the Bahamas on October 12, 1492. The landing in the Bahamas was certainly not the event of the year 1492, if only because the few who cared, on the other side of the Atlantic, did not learn about it until 1493.

How interesting, then, that 1492 has become Columbus's year, and October 12 the day of "The Discovery." Columbus himself has become a quintessential "Spaniard" or a representative of "Italy"—two rather vague entities during his lifetime. The landing has become a clear-cut event much more fixed in time than the prolonged fall of Muslim Granada, the seemingly interminable expulsion of European Jews, or the tortuous consolidation of royal power in the early Renaissance. Whereas these latter issues still appear as convoluted processes—thus the favored turf of academic specialists who break them down into an infinite list of themes for doctoral dissertations—The Discovery has lost its processual character. It has become a single and simple moment.

The creation of that historical moment facilitates the narrativization of history, the transformation of what happened into that which is said to have happened. First, chronology replaces process. All events are placed in a single line leading to the landfall. The years Columbus spent in Portugal, the knowledge he accumulated from Portuguese and North African sailors, his efforts to peddle his project to various monarchs are subsumed among the "antecedents" to The Discovery.[6] Other occurrences, such as the participation of the Pinzon brothers, are included under "the preparations," although in the time lived by the actors, that participation preceded, overlapped, and outlived the landfall. Second, as intermingled processes fade into a linear continuity, context also fades out. For instance, the making of Europe, the rise of the absolutist state, the *reconquista*, and Christian religious intransigence all spread over centuries and paralleled the invention of the Americas. These Old World transformations were not without consequences. Most notably, they created in Castile and elsewhere a number of rejects. Indeed, the first Europeans who made it to the New World were in great majority the rejects of Europe, individuals of modest means who had nothing to lose in a desperate adventure.[7] But in the narrative of The Discovery, Europe becomes a neutral and ageless essence able to function, in turn, as stage for "the preparations," as background for "the voyage," and as supportive cast in a noble epic.

The isolation of a single moment thus creates a historical "fact": on this day, in 1492, Christopher Columbus discovered the Bahamas. As a set event, void of context and marked by a fixed date, this chunk of history becomes much more manageable outside of the academic guild. It returns inevitably: one can await its millenial and prepare its commemoration. It accommodates travel agents, airlines, politicians, the media, or the states who sell it in the prepackaged forms by which the public has come to expect history to present itself for immediate consumption. It is a product of power whose label has been cleansed of traces of power.

The naming of the "fact" is itself a narrative of power disguised as innocence. Would anyone care to celebrate the "Castilian invasion of the Bahamas"? Yet this phrasing is somewhat closer to what happened on October 12, 1492, than "the discovery of America." Naming the fact thus already imposes a reading and many historical controversies boil down to who has the power to name what. To call "discovery" the first invasions of inhabited lands by Europeans is an exercise in Eurocentric power that already frames future narratives of the event so described. Contact with the West is seen as the foundation of historicity of different cultures.[8] Once discovered by Europeans, the Other finally enters the human world.

In the 1990s, quite a few observers, historians, and activists worldwide denounced the arrogance implied by this terminology during the quincentennial celebrations of Columbus's Bahamian landing. Some spoke of a Columbian Holocaust. Some proposed "conquest" instead of discovery; others preferred "encounter," which suddenly gained an immense popularity—one more testimony, if needed, of the capacity of liberal discourse to compromise between its premises and its practice.[9] "Encounter" sweetens the horror, polishes the rough edges that do not fit neatly either side of the controversy. Everyone seems to gain.

Not everyone was convinced. Portuguese historian Vitorino Magalhaes Godinho, a former minister of education, reiterated that "discovery" was an appropriate term for the European ventures of the fifteenth and sixteenth centuries, which he compares to Herschel's discovery of Uranus, and Sédillot's discovery of microbes.[10] The problem is, of course, that Uranus did not know that it existed before Herschel, and that Sédillot did not go after the microbes with a sword and a gun.

Yet more than blind arrogance is at issue here. Terminologies demarcate a field, politically and epistemologically. Names set up a field of power.[11] "Discovery" and analogous terms ensure that by just mentioning the event one enters a predetermined lexical field of clichés and predictable categories that foreclose a redefinition of the political and intellectual stakes. Europe becomes the center of "what happened." Whatever else may have happened *to* other peoples in that process is already reduced to a natural fact: they were discovered. The similarity to planets and microbes precedes their explicit mention by future historians and cabinet ministers.

For this reason, I prefer to say that Columbus "stumbled on the Bahamas," or "discovered the Antilles," and I prefer "conquest" over "discovery" to describe what happened after the landing. Such phrasings are awkward and may raise some eyebrows. They may even annoy some readers. But both the awkwardness and the fact that the entire issue can be dismissed as trivial quibbling suggests that it is not easy to subvert the very language describing the facts of the matter. For the power to decide what is trivial—and annoying—is also part of the power to decide how "what happened" becomes "that which is said to have happened."

Here again, power enters into the interface between historicity 1 and historicity 2. The triviality clause—for it is a clause, not an argument—forbids describing what happened from the point of view of some of the people who saw it happen or to whom it happened. It is a form of archival power. With the exercise of that power, "facts" become clear, sanitized.[12]

Commemorations sanitize further the messy history lived by the actors. They contribute to the continuous myth-making process that gives history its more definite shapes: they help to create, modify, or sanction the public meanings attached to historical events deemed worthy of mass celebration. As rituals that package history for public consumption, commemorations play the numbers game to create a past that seems both more real and more elementary.

Numbers matter at the end point, the consumption side of the game: the greater the number of participants in a celebration, the stronger the allusion to the multitude of witnesses for whom the mythicized event is supposed to have meant something from day one. In 1992, when millions of people celebrated a quincentennial staged by states, advertisers, and travel agents, their very mass reinforced the illusion that Columbus's contemporaries must have known—how could they not?—that October 12, 1492, was indeed a momentous event. As we have seen, it was not; and many of our contemporaries, for various reasons, said as much. But few of the 1992 celebrants could accentuate publicly the banality of that date, five hundred years before, without having to admit also that power had intervened between the event and its celebration.

The more varied the participants, the easier also the claim to world historical significance.[13] Numbers matter also as items in the calendar. Years, months, and dates present history as part of the natural cycles of the world. By packaging events within temporal sequences, commemorations adorn the past with certainty: the proof of the happening is in the cyclical inevitability of its celebration.

Cycles may vary, of course, but annual cycles provide a basic element of modern commemorations: an exact date.[14] As a tool of historical production, that date anchors the event in the present. It does so through the simultaneous production of mentions and silences. The recurrence of a predictable date severs Columbus's landfall from the context of emerging Europe on and around 1492. It obliterates the rest of the year now subsumed within a twenty-four hour segment. It imposes a silence upon all events surrounding the one being marked. A potentially endless void now encompasses everything that could be said and is not being said about 1492 and about the years immediately preceding or following.

The void, however, is not left unfilled. The fixed date alone places the event within a new frame with linkages of its own. As a fixed date, October 12 is the fetishized repository for a potentially endless list of disparate events, such as the birth of U.S. activist Dick Gregory or that of Italian tenor Luciano Pavarotti; the independence of Equatorial Guinea; the Broadway opening of the musical *Jesus Christ Superstar*; or the refusal of a Catholic monk, one Martin Luther, to repudiate assertions posted months before on the door of a church in Germany. All these events happened on October 12 of the Christian calendar, in various years from 1518 to 1971. All are likely to be acknowledged publicly by varying numbers of milestone worshippers. Each of them, in turn, can be replaced by another event judged to be equally—or more—noteworthy: Paraguay's break from Argentina in 1811, the 1976 arrest of the Chinese Gang of Four, the beginning of the German occupation of France in 1914, or the approval of the Magna Carta by Edward I of England in 1297.

The roster is theoretically expandable in any direction. If the Magna Carta is the most ancient icon mentioned here, that is because these examples have come from the institutionalized memory of what is now the West and were all indexed through Dionysius Exiguus's system. With other modes of counting and another pool of events, October 12 of the Christian calendar could overlap in any given year a number of anniversaries next to which the landing in the Bahamas would look quite recent. As arbitrary markers of time, dates link a number of dissimilar events, all equally decontextualized and equally susceptible to mythicization. The longer the list of events celebrated on the same date, the more that list looks like an answer in a trivia game. But this is precisely because celebrations trivialize the historical process (historicity 1) at the same time that they mythicize history (historicity 2).

The myth-making process does not operate evenly, however, and the preceding list suggests as much. For if—in theory—all events can be decontextualized to the same point of emptiness, in practice not all are reshaped by the same power plays and not all mean the same to new actors entering the stage and busily reformulating and appropriating the past. In short, celebrations are created, and this creation is part and parcel of the process of historical production. Celebrations straddle the two sides of historicity. They impose a silence upon the events that they ignore, and they fill that silence with narratives of power about the event they celebrate.

The reasons to celebrate Columbus Day and to do so on October 12 are now obvious to most Americans, just as the rationale behind the quincentennial was obvious to many in the West. Most advocates of these celebrations will evoke the obvious significance of "what happened" in 1492 and the no less obvious consequences of that event. But the road between then and now is no more straightforward than the relation between what happened and what is said to have happened. October 12 was certainly not a historical landmark in Columbus's day. It took centuries of battles—both petty and grandiose—and quite a bit of luck to turn it into a significant date. Further, not all those who agree now that the date and the event it indexes are important agree on the significance of its celebration. The images and debates that surround the appropriation of Columbus vary from Spain to the United States and from both Spain and the United States to Latin America, to mention only three areas treated in this chapter.[15] Constructions of Columbus and of Columbus Day vary within these areas according to time and also according to factors such as class and ethnic identification. In short, the road between then and now is itself a history of power.

An Anniversary in the Making

Columbus was not treated as a favorite hero by nascent Spain, nor was October 12 marked as a special day during his lifetime. To be sure, the landing in the Bahamas, the verified existence of an American landmass, the integration of the Caribbean in the European orbit, and the imperial reorganizations that paralleled these events imposed a symbolic reordering of the world which, in turn, contributed to the wealth of myths that now define the West—Utopia, the noble savage, the white man's burden, among others.[16] Still, it took quite a few years of intense struggles over political and economic power in Europe and the Americas for the narrative to unfold in ways that acknowledged the discovery as event and the discoverer as hero. Indeed it took a living hero, Charles V, and his pretensions to a Catholic empire stretching from Tunis to Lima and from Vienna to Vera Cruz for Columbus, then dead, to become a hero. In 1552, Francisco López de Gómara suggested to Charles that the most important event in history—after the divine Creation of the world and the Coming of Christ—was the conquest of the Americas.[17]

Even then, there was no "public" celebration. When López de Gómara wrote these lines, the Castilians who lived on American soil had already measured the gaps between the dream of a New World and the realities of their daily life under an increasingly heavy colonial bureaucracy. Columbus's first group of admirers was restricted, at best, to a few Spanish intellectuals and bureaucrats. Further, even as Spanish arts and themes gained international attention during the reign of Philip II, the sinking of the armada in 1588 had already suggested other times and priorities. By the early seventeenth century, the conquest of the Americas was as much a miscellany of efforts by French, Dutch, and British adventurers as a competition between the Iberian states. The northern Europeans who benefited most from the rise of Caribbean plantations and trans-Atlantic trade during the two centuries following Philip's reign tended to commission paintings of themselves and their families rather than writings about conquistadores. Meanwhile, among the intellectual elites of Europe, the mythicized faces of America overshadowed that of Columbus.[18]

Thus it was in the New World itself that Columbus could first emerge most strongly as myth, in the former colonies of Spain and in the United States. The United States was one of the few places where the growth of a modern public in the midst of the Enlightenment was not encumbered by images of a feudal past. There, as elsewhere, the constitution of a public domain reflected the organization of power and the development of the national state, but power was constituted differently from the way it took shape in most European countries. Citizens with a weakness for marching bands promoted celebrations and holidays more openly and often more successfully than in Europe.[19]

The Tammany Society, or Columbian Order, an otherwise clannish group of gentlemen incorporated in New York in 1789, had such a taste for public attention, parades and lavish banquets. Their list of celebrations included Washington's birthday and the Fourth of July, but also Bastille Day and other international milestones they deemed worthy of recognition. Columbus's landfall figured on their first calendar, published in 1790. More important, by what seems to be a historical accident (the joint effect of fixed dates, fund-raising opportunities, and political fortunes), their most lavish ceremony occurred on October 12, 1792. On that day, members organized a memorable banquet and erected a fourteen-foot-high monument to Columbus that they promised to illuminate annually on the anniversary of the landfall. They did not keep that promise. Still, their banquet was remembered almost a hundred years later, when new groups of worshipers searched for a North American precedent for Columbus Day.[20]

Latin America, meanwhile, kept Columbus's image alive but treated it with ambivalence until the late 1880s. Some territories fought Europe repeatedly over Columbus's remains, both literally and figuratively. Two Caribbean colonies competed with Spain for Columbus's long-dead body.[21] The independent state that emerged from Bolívar's armed struggle on the mainland claimed Columbus's name both before and after the secession of Venezuela and Ecuador from Gran Colombia. Still, even though the Latin American rejection of Spanish political tutelage did not entail a rejection of *hispanismo*, early ideologies of independence and, later, Spain's Ten Years War against Cuba (1868–1878) hampered the complete integration of Columbus into the pantheon of South American heroes.

Ethnicity—or rather, ideologies of ethnicity—added to Latin America's ambivalence toward Columbus. Latin American ideologies attribute to the New World situation an active role in the making of socio-racial categories. It is not simply that categories require new names (*criollos, zambos, mestizos*) or new ingredients under old names (*mamelucos, morenos, ladinos*); the rules by which they are devised are different from those of Europe and acknowledged as such.[22] Discourses intertwined with these rules and reproducing the Creole categories give a central role, implicit or explicit, to metaphors of "blending" in spite of the age-old denigration of certain cultural traditions and in spite of systems of stratification that manipulate the perception of phenotypes. Skewed as it was, a blending did occur.[23]

Brutal as it was also, Spanish colonization did not nearly wipe out pre-Conquest Americans in the southern landmass as the Anglos did in the north or as Spaniards themselves did in the Caribbean islands, if only because the aboriginal populations of both Mexico and the Andes were enormous. Early cultural practices often intertwined European and native elements. Early manifestations of a distinct local identity included some sense of "Indianness." Historian Stuart Schwartz draws on Fernando de Azedevo to observe that in certain regions of Brazil, "Tupí, the predominant Indian language, was more widely spoken than Portuguese . . . even by the colonists."[24] Later, political doctrines of the nineteenth century incorporated both the metaphors of a blend and the acknowledgment of the Indian, even while the organization of power kept Indians and Afro-Latins outside the decision-making process. Hence, Bolívar could declare in 1815: "We are . . . neither Indian nor European, but a species midway between the legitimate proprietors of this country and the Spanish usurpers."[25] A few decades later, nineteenth-century scientific racism did influence Latin American opinions and practices, albeit without always negating the stress on mixes rather than pure sets, on differences of degree rather than differences of kind.[26]

In short, for many reasons too complex to detail here, Latin Americans did not alienate native cultures from their myths of origin, even before the twentieth-century rise of various forms of *indigenismo.* They view themselves as *criollos* and *mestizos* of different kinds, peoples of the New World; perhaps Columbus was too much a man of the Old.[27]

In the United States, in contrast, in spite of inflated references to a melting pot, ideologies of ethnicity emphasize continuities with the *Old* World. The real natives are mainly dead or on reservations. New natives (recognizable by their hyphenated group names) are numbered by generation, and their descendants fight each other for pieces of a mythical Europe. The peculiar politics of ethnicity has proved to be a boon for Columbus's image in the United States.

Ethnicity gave Columbus a lobby, a prerequisite to public success in U.S. culture. The 1850 census reported only 3,679 individuals of Italian birth. Yet by 1866, Italian-Americans, organized by the Sharpshooters' Association of New York, celebrated the landfall and, within three years, annual festivities were being held in Philadelphia, St. Louis, Boston, Cincinnati, New Orleans, and San Francisco on or around October 12.[28] Italians and Spaniards were just not enough, however, to turn this celebration into a national practice. Fortunately, ethnicity gave Columbus a second—and more numerous—group of lobbyists, Irish-Americans.

By 1850, there were already 962,000 Americans claiming Irish descent. Many of them regrouped in organizations like the Knights of Columbus, a fraternal society for Catholic males founded in 1881. In less than ten years, community support and the institutional patronage of the Catholic church swelled the Knights' membership. As the association spread in the northeast with the backing of prominent Irish-Americans, it increasingly emphasized the shaping of "citizen culture."[29] Columbus played a leading role in making citizens out of these immigrants. He provided them with a public example of Catholic devotion and civic virtue, and thus a powerful rejoinder to the cliché that allegiance to Rome preempted the Catholics' attachment to the United States. In New Haven, the 1892 celebration of the landing attracted some forty thousand people—including six thousand Knights and a thousand-piece band conducted by the musical director of West Point—in a joint celebration of holiness and patriotism.[30]

The success of these festivities was not due solely to Catholic-Americans' desire for acceptance, nor was the cult of Columbus limited to Catholics. The introduction of history into the school curriculum as a required subject in the early nineteenth century and its slow growth before the Civil War also contributed to familiarizing a larger audience with Columbus.[31] So did the few biographical sketches published in the first half of the century. Nevertheless, the Catholic connection was crucial in that Catholics provided the bodies that made possible the mass celebrations of Columbus Day before the 1890s. By the 1890s, Italian and Irish efforts to promote Columbus Day in the United States coincided with—and ultimately were subsumed within—the production of two mass media events, the international celebrations of the quadricentennial of the Bahamas landfall respectively sponsored by Spain and the United States.

The Castilian and the Yankee

The second half of the nineteenth century saw an unprecedented attention to the systematic management of public discourse in countries that combined substantial working classes and wide electoral franchises. With the realization that "the public"—this rather vague presumption of the first bourgeois revolutions—indeed existed, government officials, entrepreneurs, and intellectuals joined in the planned production of traditions that cut across class identities and reinforced the national state. Nationalist parades multiplied in Europe, while government imposed a daily homage to the flag in public schools in the United States. International fairs that attracted millions of visitors to London, Paris, and Philadelphia; academic conferences (such as the first congress of Orientalists in 1873), and official commemorations (such as the 1880 invention of Bastille Day, in France) taught the new masses who they were, in part by telling them who they were not.

Socialists, anarchists, and working-class political activists replied in kind by publicizing their own heroes and promoting celebrations such as May Day. Public history was in the air.[32]

This fast-moving fin-de-siècle era caught Spain in a state of decline. Torn by factional feuds, outflanked in Europe by nearly all the Atlantic states, threatened in the Americas by the economic incursions of Britain, the influence of the United States, and the constant fear of losing Cuba, Spain was in dire need of a moral and political uplift.[33] Conservative leader Antonio Cánovas del Castillo, architect of the Bourbon Restoration and a historian in his own right, made of Columbus and The Discovery the consummate metaphors for this anticipated revitalization.

Interest in Columbus had grown in the 1800s. The number of biographical sketches published in Europe and the Americas increased significantly after the 1830s. So did various suggestions of a quadricentennial in the 1880s. Cánovas turned this growing interest into an extravaganza: a political and diplomatic crusade, an economic venture, a spectacle to be consumed by Spain and the world for the sheer sake of its pageantry. The commemoration became a powerful tool with which the politician-historian and his quadricentennial junta of academics and bureaucrats wrote a narrative of The Discovery with Spain as the main character. In the words of its most thorough chronicler, the Spanish quadricentennial was "the apex of the Restoration."[34]

Spain spent more than two and a half million pesetas and four years of preparation on the celebration. Various cities were refurbished, monuments erected, and pavilions built on the model of recent international exhibitions.[35] A yearlong series of events led to grandiose ceremonies in October and November of 1892 that involved the Spanish royal family and many foreign dignitaries. On October 9, Cánovas, his wife, and members of the royal family took part in a mock exploration off the Andalusian coast with escort ships from twelve foreign countries. At least twenty-four countries participated officially in the Spanish quadricentennial.[36] Replicas of Columbus's boats sailed across the Atlantic. For a few weeks, Spain was at the center of the world. Parades in Madrid and Seville were echoed in Havana and Manila, and officials from the most powerful western countries paid homage to Spain.

The huge international participation was due, in a large part, to Cánovas's careful packaging of both the celebration and its object, the discovery itself. He sold the quadricentennial not only as pageantry but as a challenge to the most enlightened minds, a yearlong symposium on past and present policy, on the role of Spain in the world, on Western civilization, and on the relevance of history. In a series of moves that anticipated the 1992 quincentennial, the quadricentennial junta set up a series of intellectual activities that legitimized the celebration.[37]

The junta created at least one serious academic journal, influenced others, dealt with learned societies, and commissioned research that still inspires European and American studies. From February 1891 to May 1892, more than fifty public lectures were delivered in the Ateneo de Madrid alone. Many titles show the role of the quadricentennial in shaping the categories and themes under which the conquest of the Americas is still discussed: the differential impact of various colonial systems on conquered populations, the accuracy of the Black Legend, the cultural legacies of pre-Conquest Americans, Spain's treatment of Columbus, Columbus's role as compared to that of other European explorers, his exact landing place, his exact burial place, etc.[38] These activities not only influenced participating academics, they also shaped the general public's perception of what was at stake. First, they made the discovery and Columbus worthy of increased public attention by making them objects of learned discourse. Second, they gave anyone who granted that attention—individuals, parties, or states—an apparently neutral ground to celebrate in spite of conflicting connotations and purposes.

Connotations and purposes varied widely. Spanish urban crowds took the quadricentennial as the homage to Spain it was in part meant to be, the symbol of an impending revitalization. Journalist Angel Stor spoke in the name of many when he wrote: "There is in the discovery of America a character much greater than Isabella and Ferdinand the Catholic . . . much greater than Columbus himself, for never was an individual able to do what a people can. This character is Spain, the true protagonist of this wonderful epic."[39]

Cánovas's narrative was not too different from that of Stor. He saw in the celebration a unique occasion to reinforce Spain's presence west of the Atlantic and—to a lesser extent—in Europe. But he also used the commemoration to consolidate his personal power. The quadricentennial made him a supporting character of Spain's story, the necessary shadow of the protagonist. In a political context marked by Spain's first experiment with "universal" (male) suffrage and nearly obsessional fears of losing face in Europe and elsewhere, Cánovas came out of the celebrations as a bona fide representative of the nation and a guarantor of her honor.

Honor was not the only stake. To a large extent, Spain's quadricentennial also aimed to create a space for a new conquest of the Americas. Although token gifts—such as schools and dispensaries—were made to the Philippines, the celebrants' eyes were on the other side of the Atlantic. Many Spanish leaders felt the need to reinforce commercial and cultural ties with Latin America in the face of U.S. gains. At the same time, those who wanted Spanish olives or wine to enter the United States saw in the celebrations an occasion to establish contact with North American firms and agencies.

U.S. brokers, in turn, wanted contact but only on their own terms. Theirs was the only country whose name contained a continent (South Africa came much later), and whose imperial destiny was unfolding along manifest tracks. Thus if for Spain, the quadricentennial was an occasion to authenticate past splendors and imagine future glories, for many in the United States it was an opportunity to verify and celebrate their present course. Accordingly, U.S. officials paid lip service to Cánovas's festivities, but invested their energy in *their* quadricentennial, the World's Columbian Exposition of Chicago.

The Chicago Exposition actually opened in 1893, but by then, historical accuracy and even Columbus himself had become quite secondary. The intellectual aspect of the event barely mattered in spite of contributions from Harvard's Peabody Museum and the Smithsonian Institution and the presence of then-rising star Franz Boas. Henry Adams later wrote in his *Education*: "The Exposition denied philosophy . . . [S]ince Noah's Ark, no such Babel of loose and ill-jointed, such vague and ill-defined and unrelated thoughts and half-thoughts and experimental outcries . . . had ruffled the surface of the Lakes."[40]

Compared to Madrid 1892, Chicago 1893 was no intellectual event. The main point was money: to be spent and to be made. United States appropriations for the 1892 celebration in Madrid were a mere $25,000, thus one-tenth of U.S. appropriations for the 1889 fair in Paris and a trifle compared to the $5.8 million for the Chicago Exposition.[41] Paris 1889 and, closer to home, the 1876 centennial of U.S. independence in Philadelphia had proved to North American entrepreneurs that international fairs generated profits. By the late 1870s, consensus was reached among the likes of W. Rockefeller, C. Vanderbilt, J. P. Morgan, and W. Waldorf Astor that the United States needed one more of these money-making events. That it occurred in Chicago one year too late was the combined result of accidents and false starts among bureaucrats and investors. That it bore Columbus's name and included a Spanish Infanta as the guest of honor were merely additional attractions.

Circumstantial as he was to his own occasion, Columbus gained a lot from Chicago. Commemorations feed on numbers and the 1893 quadricentennial was a display of the U.S. appetite for size: more participating countries, more acreage, more exhibits, more money than any fair the world had known. Chicago won the numbers game—second only to Paris for attendance—and provided Columbus his most successful celebration to date: $28.3 million in expenses; $28.8 million in receipts; 21.5 million people in attendance—and no protest in the local records. Some Spanish journalists ridiculed what they saw as a vulgar carnival, but the Chicago numbers spoke for themselves. Columbus was the wrapping for an extravagant Yankee bazaar; but in the end, the bazaar was so big that the wrapping was noticed.

Latin America certainly noticed. To be sure, Columbus's metamorphosis into a Yankee hero, the lone ranger of the western seas, looked somewhat banal outside Chicago. Still, viewed from the far south, the fair belonged to a political and economic series from which it drew its symbolism. The Columbus story written in Chicago overlapped with the ongoing narrative of conquest that U.S. power was busily writing in the lands of this hemisphere. What was said to have happened in 1492 legitimized what was actually happening in the early 1890s. In 1889, Secretary of State James Gillepsie Blaine, one of the promoters of the celebration, had convened the first meeting of American states in Washington.[42] In 1890, Minor C. Keith acquired eight hundred thousand acres of public land in Costa Rica, the U.S. Congress passed the McKinley Tariff, and U.S. entrepreneurs controlled 80 percent of Cuban sugar exports. In 1891 U.S. admiral Bancroft Gherardi threatened to seize part of Haiti and the U.S. Navy prepared for war against Chile. In 1892, the postmaster of the

United States, acting as a private citizen-broker, bought the entire foreign debt of the Dominican Republic. Four centuries after Spain, the United States was taking over. The path was the same: first the Caribbean, then the continental landmass. Columbus as Yankee looked somewhat more real, if not necessarily less foolish, in light of that ongoing expansion.[43]

Europe also noticed. The Pan-American strategy was designed in part to block European incursions in the hemisphere. In the 1880s, British investments in South America exceeded those of the United States. The French also were perceived as a threat until the 1889 collapse of their canal project. Even German and Italian ventures, relatively small, were watched with suspicion from North America. Thus, from 1890 to the end of the fair, Europeans were told repeatedly how to read Columbus and what this new reading meant for the hemisphere.

The imposition of this new reading required the production of a number of silences. Since some traces could not be erased, their historical significance had to be reduced. They became inconsequential or significant only in light of the new interpretation. Thus, the official guide to the fair dismissed as meaningless the first 280 years of Euro-American history: the history of this hemisphere prior to 1776 was a mere "preparatory period" to the rise of the United States. The meaning of the discovery could be measured by the number of bushels of wheat that the United States now produced and the length of its railways. Shunning Europe and Latin America in the same stroke, the guide added: "Most fitting it is, therefore, that the people of the greatest nation on the continent discovered by Christopher Columbus, should lead in the celebration of the Four Hundredth Anniversary of that event."[44]

Even U.S. citizens were told in unmistakable terms what Columbus was not about, lest working-class Irish and, especially, Italian families use him as a shield to hide their own highly suspect invasion. The number of immigrants from Europe had doubled between 1860 and 1893. At the same time, the countries of origins were increasingly non-English speaking areas of what passed then for "Southern Europe": Italy, Russia, Poland, Bohemia, and other lands of doubtful whiteness. By 1890, the number of Italian immigrants was over three hundred thousand.

In the context of that migration, ideas suggesting the biological inferiority of the "southern" immigrants and the threat they constituted to the "future race" of the United States became widespread. Progressive journals taking the new immigrants' side published articles with titles such as "Are the Italians a Dangerous Class?"[45] Two years after the number of Italians passed the three hundred thousand mark, railroad magnate Chauncey M. Depew, having conceded in a speech that Columbus Day belonged "not to America, but to the world," went on to warn against "unhealthy immigration," urging U.S. citizens to "quarantine against disease, pauperism and crime."[46] It took only a centennial for similar propositions to reappear in California and Florida in the 1990s. But by then, the diatribes were directed at Mexican and Caribbean immigrants; the Italians and the Russians had been integrated in the white melting pot.

Vanity notwithstanding, those who wrote the script for Chicago could not control all the possible readings of that script. Their triumph was due, in part, to their taking Columbus further out of context than did their predecessors. Once that was done, however, Columbus was not theirs alone. Successful celebrations decontextualize successfully the events they celebrate, but in so doing they open the door to competitive readings of these events. The richer the ritual, the easier it is for subsequent performers to change parts of the script or to impose new interpretations. The recent controversies about the quincentennial celebrations of the Bahamas landing were possible in part because of the extravagant investments—both material and symbolic—of the celebrants.

But the reach of these controversies was also increased by the significance of past celebrations. As rituals of a special kind, commemorations build upon each other, and each celebration raises the stake for the next one. Cánovas's fiesta and the earlier parades of Italian- and Irish-Americans had unwittingly promoted the Chicago fair. The Chicago fair, in turn, was read by some immigrants as an acknowledgment of their presence in the melting pot—clearly an unexpected effect from the point of view of the magnates. From then on, Catholic Americans felt partly vindicated by their hero's national recognition.

By the 1890s, the appropriation of Columbus in the United States truly became a national phenomenon. Narratives were produced that rewrote a past meant to certify the inevitability of a Columbian connection. Ethnic and religious leaders, counties and municipalities started to look for traces of Columbus in their origins, silencing prior narratives, busily creating others. By the end of the decade, for instance, it had become public knowledge that the Ohio town of Columbus was named after the Discoverer. Yet the major documents that record the establishment of Columbus as seat of the state government of Ohio do not make any reference to the Genoese navigator. Columbus the man was not mentioned in the original bill, or in the *Journal of the House* when the bill was signed and sent to the Senate. Nor was he mentioned when the bill was amended a few years later. In 1816, Governor Worthington, addressing the Ohio legislature, simply stated that Columbus had become the permanent seat of local government without mention of Columbus the man. In that same year, *The Ohio Gazetteer* did make an allusion to the United States as a "Columbian Republic," but its descriptions of Columbus the town do not evoke the Genoese sailor. Nor do successive editions. Further descriptions or histories of both the town and the state from the 1830s to the 1850s are equally silent about a connection between Columbus, Ohio, and Columbus, the Genoese. Even a comprehensive history of the town published in 1873 does not mention such a connection.[47] In short, as late as 1873, the connection between Columbus, Ohio, and Christopher Columbus was historically irrelevant.

Yet by 1892, in the euphoria that surrounded the Chicago fair, historians were listing Columbus, Ohio, as an obvious proof of Columbus's wide recognition in the United States.[48] A century later, for the launching of AmeriFlora '92, a quincentennial event set in Columbus, President Bush reaffirmed the inevitability of a connection by then firmly established:

> It is most fitting that this special event has been designated an official Quincentennial Project by the Jubilee Commission. To be held in Columbus, Ohio—the largest city in the world named after this great explorer—AmeriFlora '92 will celebrate the rich cultural heritage of not only the lands he discovered but also the continent from which he travelled.[49]

The final measure of Chicago's success is the extent to which it naturalized Columbus. A century after the fair, fourteen states other than Ohio had towns named Columbus, and a number of Columbias filled the U.S. landscape.[50] Yet President Bush's reference to the cultural heritage of American Indians aside, this more American Columbus was also a whiter Columbus. All hyphens are not equal in the pot that does not melt. The second part of the compound—Irish-*American*, Jewish-*American*, Anglo-*American*—always emphasizes whiteness. The first part only measures compatibility with the second at a given historical moment.[51] Thus, as he became more American, Columbus had to become whiter, in spite of the anti-Italian racism prevailing at the time of the Chicago fair. As Columbus became whiter he also contributed to the whitening of the people who claimed him as part of their past, further opening to multiple interpretations the narrative officialized at Chicago. The very success of the fair created an ideological breach in the vision of the United States proposed by some of its promoters.

Three years after the fair, determined to muddle the script broadcast in Chicago, Italians in New York founded the Sons of Columbus Legion, which celebrated Columbus Day the following year.[52] Their efforts mingled with those of the Irish, though not always by way of formal collaboration. The Knights, in particular, worked hard for their chosen ancestor. As Irish-Americans spread through the country with the full benefits of white status, the Knights petitioned successive state legislatures to make October 12 a legal holiday. By 1912, they were victorious. Columbus himself, further out of the context of 1492 Europe, became more Irish than ever—until Italian-Americans made new gains in the continuing contest for racial and historical legitimacy with the mass migrations that followed each of two world wars.[53]

Latin Americans also appropriated Columbus in unexpected ways, skewing plans made in both Madrid and Washington. The Spanish government had promoted emigration to South America in the late nineteenth century, as part of a larger movement to promote *hispanismo* in the region. From Madrid's viewpoint, attachment to Spanish culture and veneration of a Spanish heritage would counteract the growing political and economic influence of the United States. Madrid's promotion of Columbus Day as the day of Hispanity in the colonies and former colonies fitted well into this scheme, which was in obvious conflict with the dominant image of Columbus promoted in the United States. Latin Americans, who participated in both quadricentennials, resolved these conflicts in their own favor.

The image of Columbus with a cowboy hat escorting Wells Fargo wagons was simply not convincing south of Texas, but it

Columbus's landing in Haiti viewed by Haitian painter J. Chéry

did challenge the Columbus as Renaissance monk favored by Cánovas's Spain. In trying to make of Columbus a North American, the Chicago fair made of him a man of the Americas. That was due to a confusion of tongues, deliberate only in part. From the U.S. viewpoint, turning the discoverer into an "American" was equivalent to putting on him a "made in USA" label, for the United States *is* America.[54] Latin Americans, for their part, could not appropriate Columbus from Spain. Their cultural heritage, their views on blending, their semiperipheral position in the world economy simply did not lead to this take-over: they had neither the means nor the will. Thus, they had watched from the sidelines the Americanization of Columbus. But that Americanization had different implications for the Latin Americans. For them, the hemisphere is not the exclusive property of *norteamericanos*. "American" means neither "gringo" nor "Yankee"—at least not necessarily. An "American" Columbus belonged to the hemisphere. Adding their own line to two different scripts, Latin Americans forced both the Spanish and the U.S. figures into their "blending" discourse. Throughout Latin America, October 12 became either the day to honor Spanish influence or to honor its opposite or, more often, to celebrate a blending of the two: Discovery Day, the Day of the Americas, or simply *El Día de la Raza*, the Day of the Race, the day of the people—a day for ourselves, however defined, for ethnicity however constructed.[55] *La Raza* has in Merida or Cartagena accents unknown in San Juan or in Santiago de Chile, and Columbus wears a different hat in each of these places.[56]

October 12, Revisited

Would the real Columbus please stand up? The problem is, of course, in the injunction itself, as we should have learned from the flurry of activities, pro and con, that surrounded the quincentennial of the Bahamas landing.

The 1992 quincentennial benefited from a material and ideological apparatus that was simply unthinkable at the time of the Chicago fair. With worldwide changes in the nature of "the public," with the sophistication of communication techniques, public history is often now a tale of sheer power clothed in electronic innocence and lexical clarity. Image makers can produce on the screen, on the page, or on the streets, shows, slogans, or rituals that seem more authentic to the masses than the original events they mimic or celebrate. The speed at which commodities, information, and individuals travel and, conversely, the decreasing significance of face-to-face interaction influence both the kinds of communities people wish to be part of and the kinds of communities to which they think they belong.

Professional manipulators with all sorts of good intentions use this tension—and its historical components—as a springboard.

A flag, a memorial, a museum exhibit, or an anniversary can become the center of a living theater with historical pretensions and worldwide audiences. The production of history for mass consumption in the form of commercial and political rituals has thus become increasingly manipulative in spite of the participation of professional historians as consultants to these various ventures. Not surprisingly, as 1992 neared, commercial, intellectual, and political brokers prepared to turn the quincentennial into a global extravaganza.

To some extent, they were successful. The Spanish government did its best to duplicate Cánovas's quadricentennial extravaganza with an updated technology. The U.S. government set up a Jubilee Commission and the Library of Congress a Quincentenary Series. Parisian intellectuals activated their ghost writers to produce as many books as possible with Columbus or 1492 in their titles. Columbus movies, both European and American, were probably more successful in reaching a larger audience from Winnipeg to Calcutta than the Parisian titles or the plethora of articles published in U.S. academic journals. Televised dramatizations of the Bahamas landing were seen at least on three continents.

Yet in spite of these extraordinary means of historical production, the quincentennial was a flop compared to the celebrations of the 1890s. Transformations in the nature of the public, in the ties that bind collectivities, and in the speed and weight of electronic communications produced contradictory results. While masses everywhere are increasingly accessible targets, the retorts produced by dissenting minorities also reach a wider audience. While the public today is increasingly international, it is also increasingly fragmented.

This fragmentation cuts both ways. In 1991–92, many U.S. advertisers were ready to reap a quincentennial bonus from the new Hispanic market. They planned to adorn with Columbian images an arsenal of products from coffee and potato chips to sport shirts and cigarettes. They designed campaigns to make Columbus sell cars and furniture, on the model of the mattress sales that honor Washington's birthday. But it took a few weeks for the loud campaign of a few Hispanic activists protesting the commemoration to burst open the Hispanic market. With Columbus persona non grata among Spanish speakers and The Discovery redefined as conquest, many advertisers dropped their Hispanic quincentennial campaigns.

In retrospect, the most striking feature of the quincentennial was the loudness of dissenting voices worldwide. For varying reasons and in various degrees, native and black Americans, Latino-Americans, African, Caribbean, and Asian leaders denounced the celebration of the conquest or tried to redirect the narrative of The Discovery. The impact of such protests and addenda varied, but celebrants everywhere had to take them into account. In a bold move, Spain's economic and political magnates apologized for the first time for the 1492 persecution of the Jews and called on Sephardics to join in the extravaganza. Some Jewish-American lobbies happily jumped on the Columbus's quincentennial bandwagon, but the quiet dissent of many more constituencies in the United States and elsewhere defied claims that what happened in 1492 was as clear as the promoters suggested.

This multiplication of voices and perspectives made it impossible for the promoters of 1992 to even approximate the relative smoothness of Madrid 1892 and Chicago 1893. Both Madrid and Chicago were, as we have seen, about their own present. But both Madrid and Chicago could effectively talk about that present by packaging a past that seemed fixed and given: on October 12, 1492, Christopher Columbus discovered the New World. That past was not so clear by 1992. Reenactments notwithstanding, what actually happened on October 12, 1492, was largely irrelevant to the quincentennial debates, certainly not at the core of either research or contention. Most contestants and observers—and quite a few celebrants—agreed that the significance of that day arose from what happened after it.

But what happened after is no longer a simple story. Between us and Columbus stand the millions of men and women who succeeded him in crossing the Atlantic by choice or by force, and the millions of others who witnessed these crossings from either side of the ocean. They, in turn, provided their own visions of what happened and their successors continue to modify the script, with both their words and their deeds. Narratives that straddle eras and continents continuously replace the Bahamas landfall in the present of its own aftermath. Thus while Columbus's landfall made possible world history as we know it, post-Columbian history continues to define the very terms under which to describe that landfall. Post-Columbian history up to the 1890s made possible the Chicago narrative, but the history of our times makes it impossible to repeat Chicago. What happened and what is said to have happened mix inextricably the two sides of historicity.

Does the label "Native American," unclaimed in the 1800s, redress a historical mistake? It does, to the extent that it avoids a confusion with South Asians and restores their chronological priority to the only peoples who can claim to be indigenous of this hemisphere. Native activists now, rather than anthropologists, speak in the name of the former "Indians." But exchanging the name imposed by the Castilians for that bequeathed by Vespucci can surely not mean starting with a clean slate. While self-naming may indicate a willingness to enter history as subjects, the concrete pool from which to choose both names and subjectivities is not immeasurable. The collective identity in the name of which Native Americans from Arizona to the Amazon defied the quincentennial is itself a late post-Columbian development.

But so is the collective identity of the Euro-Americans who claim Columbus as an ancestor. And so, for that matter, is the national consciousness that colored the quincentennial in Spain or in Italy. The inability to step out of history in order to write or rewrite it applies to all actors and narrators. That some ambiguities are more obvious in Arizona and in Belém than in Chicago, Madrid, or Paris has much more to do with unequal control over the means of historical production than with the inherent objectivity of a particular group of narrators. This does not suggest that history is never honest but rather that it is always confusing because of its constituting mixes.

If history is as messy as I think it is for its subjects, the "real" Columbus would have no final reading of the events he generated—certainly not at the time of their occurrence. Genoese by birth, Mediterranean by training, Castilian by necessity, Cristobal Colón had no final word on things much more trivial than his landfall. He contradicted himself many times—much like other historical actors, sometimes more than most. He left some blanks on purpose; he left others because he did not know better; and yet others because he could not do otherwise. In Columbus's travel journal, there is a description of the first sighting of land on Thursday October 11, 1492. In his log entry for the day Columbus hints about the tense evening, the long night that followed, the first views of land at two in the morning. "At two hours after midnight, land appeared, from which they were about two leagues distant. They hauled down the sails . . . passing time until daylight Friday," when they reached an islet and descended.[57]

There is no clear-cut milestone in the log.[58] It was a messy night—not Thursday any more, but not yet Friday. At any rate, there is no separate entry in Columbus's journal for Friday, October 12, 1492.

The Presence in the Past

5

They came long before Columbus. For reasons we can only guess, they had stopped in this arid land where their sole sources of water were gigantic sinkholes nature had carved into the limestone. Here, in the province of Chichén, they had built their temples between two of these wells. They had surveyed the skies from these heights, master astronomers, aware of mathematical secrets that Europeans barely guessed. They were practiced warriors. Most strikingly, they were devout. They had kept one well for themselves and given to their gods the deep one with the green waters.

I knew all these stories. I had done my homework before coming to Maya land. Now, I wanted something real. Hunting, my eyes descended the limestone walls eighty feet down into the well. This was the Cenote of Sacrifice, the Sacred Well of Chichén Itzá.

The still green waters did not speak of war and murder. Not a ripple of blood disturbed their cool surface. Here and there a dead leaf, dropped from the air far above, left a patch of darker green over the underground lake. But there was no movement on the water surface. Here, the past was hidden by a verdant coat of silence.

I coughed nervously, sweeping the water with my binoculars. I was in search of evidence. I was eager to see a corpse, a skull, some bones, any gruesome trace of history. But the belly of the earth uttered only the echo of my cough.

Yet history had to be there. Below the water, hundreds of corpses melted into the earth—women, men, and children, many of them thrown alive to deities now forgotten, for reasons now murkier than the bottom of this well. Stories about these sacrifices spanned at least ten centuries. Scavengers of all sorts—colonists, diplomats, warriors, and archaeologists—had unearthed the proofs behind these narratives. Still, I felt disappointed: there was nothing here to touch, nothing to see except a dormant green liquid.

I retraced my steps along the ancient path to the central pyramid. That, at least, seemed concrete, and I had not yet made the journey to the top. Up there, as in the well, history required bodily donations. I had to pay my part of sweat for the encounter to be sincere. Stoically, I climbed the stairs, all 354 of them, and I ventured into the ruins. Inside, for a long time, I ran my fingers on the walls, probing mysteries unresolved, longing for recognition. But as much as I was touched by the magnificence of the structure, I never came to feel that I was touching history. I climbed down the pyramid, careful not to look into the void, blaming myself for this failure to communicate with a past so magnificently close.

Many exotic lands later, I understood better my trip to Chichén Itzá. History was alive and I had heard its sounds elsewhere. From Rouen to Santa Fe, from Bangkok to Lisbon, I had touched ghosts suddenly real, I had engaged people far remote in time and in space. Distance was no barrier. History did not need to be mine in order to engage me. It just needed to relate to someone, anyone. It could not just be The Past. It had to be someone's past.

In my first trip to the Yucatan, I had failed to meet the peoples whose past Chichén Itzá was. I could not resuscitate a single mathematician viewing the skies from the Caracol, a single sacrificial victim pushed toward the green waters. And I knew even less then how to relate the Mayas of today to the architects of the pyramids. That, no doubt, was my fault, my lack of imagination, or a shortfall of erudition. At any rate, I had missed a vital connection to the present. I had honored the past, but the past was not history.

Slavery in Disneyland

The controversies about EuroDisney had not yet faded when the mammoth transnational revealed its plans for Disney's America, a new amusement park to be built in northern Virginia. Aware that environmental and historical tourism are among the fastest growing branches of that industry, Disney emphasized the historical themes of the park. Afro-American slavery was one of them.

Protests immediately erupted. Black activists accused Disney of turning slavery into a tourist attraction. Others intimated that white corporate types were not qualified to address the subject. Others wondered whether the subject should be addressed at all. Disney's chief imageer tried to calm the public: activists need not worry, we guarantee the exhibit to be "painful, disturbing and agonizing."

William Styron, a popular novelist, author of such best-sellers as *Sophie's Choice* and *The Confessions of Nat Turner*, denounced Disney's plans in the pages of *The New York Times*.[1] Styron, whose grandmother owned slaves, asserted that Disney could only "mock a theme as momentous as slavery" because "slavery cannot be represented in exhibits." Whatever the images displayed and the technical means deployed, the artifacts of cruelty and oppression "would have to be fraudulent" because they would be inherently unable to "define such a stupendous experience." The moral dilemmas of many whites and especially the suffering of blacks would be missing from the exhibit, not because such experiences could not be displayed, but because their very display would beget a cheap romanticism. Styron concluded: "At Disney's Virginia park, the slave experience would permit visitors a shudder of horror before they turned away, smug and self-exculpatory, from a world that may be dead but has not really been laid to rest."

When I first read these lines, I wished a practicing historian had written them. Then it occurred to me that few historians could have done so. Indeed, my second thought was for another novelist writing about yet a third one.

In a story often evoked in debates about authenticity, Jorge Luis Borges imagines that a French novelist of the 1930s produces a novel that is word for word a fragmentary version of *Don Quixote de la Mancha*. Borges insists: Pierre Ménard did not copy *Don Quixote*, nor did he try to be Miguel de Cervantes. He rejected the temptation to mimic both Cervantes's life and style as too facile. He achieved his feat after many drafts, at the end of which his text was the same as that of Cervantes.[2] Is that second novel a fake and why? Is it, indeed, a "second" novel? What is the relationship between Ménard's work and that of Cervantes?

Disney dropped its plans for the Virginia park, much less because of the controversy about slavery than in reaction to other kinds of pressure.[3] Still, the plans for the park can be interpreted as a parody of Borges's parody. Indeed, read against one another, the respective projects of the transnational and of Borges's fictitious writer provide a pointed lesson about the fourth moment of historical production, the moment of retrospective significance.[4]

Neither in the case of the park nor in that of the book is empirical exactitude a primary issue. Disney could gather all the relevant facts for its planned exhibits, just as the words in Ménard's final draft were exactly the same as those in Cervantes's *Don Quixote*. Indeed, the Disney corporation flaunted its use of historians as paid consultants—proof, as it were, of its high regard for empirical exactitude. The limitless possibility for errors remained but, other things being equal, one could imagine a version of Disney's America as empirically sound as the average history book.

Styron, who wrote a controversial novel about slavery, knows this. He expresses concerns about empirical issues, but his emphasis is elsewhere. Styron even admits, although reluctantly, that Disney could duplicate the mood of the times. Modern imageers have enough means to stage virtual reality. Yet Styron remains indignant, and it is this indignation that helps him stir his way through his previous objections toward a conclusion that follows the tourists until *after* they turn away.

Deconstruction's most famous line may be Jacques Derrida's sentence: *il n'y a pas de hors-texte.* How literally can we take the claim that there is no life beyond the text? To be sure, we may decide not to get out of the amusement park. We can argue that if Disney's imageers had produced the virtual reality of slavery, the paying tourist would have been projected in history. It would have mattered little then, if that projection were a short or even short-sighted representation. Similarly, we may tell Borges that the issue of authenticity is irrelevant and that both novels are the same, however awkward this phrasing. Yet if such answers are unsatisfactory, then, we need to get out the text(s) and look for life after Disney. And, I would argue, getting out the text enables us also to get out of the tyranny of the facts. The realization that historical production is itself historical is the only way out of the false dilemmas posed by positivist empiricism and extreme formalism.

In the subtext of Styron's objections is a fundamental premise: Disney's primary public was to be white middle-class Americans. They are the ones for whom the park was planned, if only because their aggregate buying power makes them the prime consumers of such historical displays. They are the ones most likely to have plunged into the fake agony of Disney's virtual reality. Styron does not spell out this premise, expressed only through innuendos. Perhaps he wants to avoid accusations of bending to "political correctness." Perhaps he wants to avoid the issue of collective white guilt. He is careful to suggest, quite rightly in my view, that the exhibit would have misrepresented the experiences of both blacks and whites.

The value of a historical product cannot be debated without taking into account both the context of its production and the context of its consumption.[5] It may be no accident that this insight comes from a popular novelist in the pages of a mass market daily. At any rate, few academic historians would have set the problem in these terms; for academic historians are trained to neglect the very actor that Styron or *The New York Times* cannot ignore, the public. The nature of that public is at the center of Styron's objections.

To phrase the argument in these terms is immediately to reintroduce history or, better, to refuse to get out of it for the seraphic comfort of the text or the immutable security of The Past. Styron refuses to separate the history of slavery from that of the United States after the Civil War. He devotes just a few lines to the time after Union cavalry men invaded his grandmother's plantation, to the fate of the ex-slaves, to Jim Crow laws and the Ku Klux Klan, and to illiteracy among blacks. He adds, almost in passing, that this post-slavery period is what actually haunts him.

The time that elapsed between the demise of slavery and the planning of the Virginia park shaped the meaning of Disney's representation of slavery. Time here is not mere chronological continuity. It is the range of disjointed moments, practices, and symbols that thread the historical relations between events and narrative. Borges's Ménard makes this complex point in simpler terms: "It is not in vain that three hundred years have passed, charged with the most complex happenings—among them, to mention only one, that same *Don Quixote*."[6] We could parody him further: it is not irrelevant that a century of complex occurrences has passed in the United States, while slavery hangs on as an issue. That U.S. slavery has both officially ended, yet continues in many complex forms—most notably institutionalized racism and the cultural denigration of blackness—makes its representation particularly burdensome in the United States. Slavery here is a ghost, both the past and a living presence; and the problem of historical representation is how to represent that ghost, something that is and yet is not.

I disagree, therefore, with Styron's comment that the Holocaust Museum in Washington is illuminating and that displays of slavery in Virginia would be obscene because of some inherent difference in magnitude or complexity between the two phenomena described. That argument rests on the assumption of a fixed past. But the cost accounting of historical suffering makes sense only as a presence projected in the past. That presence ("look at me now") and its projection ("I have suffered") function together as a new exhibit for claims and gains in a changing present. Many European Jews who condemn projects of parody at Auschwitz or elsewhere in Poland, Germany, France, or the Soviet Union deploy the same moral arguments that Styron uses against mock plantations today in Virginia.

Do displays of Jewish genocide run greater risks of being obscene in Poland than in Virginia? The illuminating value of the Holocaust Museum in Washington may be as much tied to the current situation of American Jews as to the real bodies in and around Auschwitz. Indeed, many Holocaust survivors are not sure that such a museum would be illuminating at Auschwitz itself. The crux of the matter is the here and now, the relations between the events described and their public representation in a specific historical context.

These relations debunk the myth of The Past as a fixed reality and the related view of knowledge as a fixed content. They also force us to look at the purpose of this knowledge. What is scary about tourist attractions representing slavery in the United States is not so much that the tourists would learn the wrong facts, but rather, that touristic representations of the facts would induce among them the wrong reaction. Obviously, the word "wrong" has different meanings here. It denotes inaccuracy in the first case. In the second, it suggests an immoral or, at least, unauthentic behavior.

Cascardi suggests that "authenticity is not a type or degree of knowledge, but a relationship to what is known."[7] To say that "what is known" must include the present will seem self-evident, but it may be less obvious that historical authenticity resides not in the fidelity to an alleged past but in an honesty vis-à-vis the present as it re-presents that past. When we imagine Disney's project and visualize a line of white tourists munching on chewing gum and fatty food, purchasing tickets for the "painful, disturbing and agonizing" experience promised by television ads, we are not into The Past. And we should not ask these tourists to be true to that past: they were not responsible for slavery. What is obscene in that image is not a relation to The Past, but the dishonesty of that relation as it would happen in our present. The trivialization of slavery—and of the suffering it caused—inheres in that present, which includes both racism and representations of slavery. Ironically, a visit by a Klan member actively promoting racial inequality would have stood a better chance of authenticity. At least, it would not have trivialized slavery.

One understands why many practicing historians kept silent. The denunciation of slavery in a presentist mode is easy. Slavery was bad, most of us would agree. But, presentism is by definition anachronistic. To condemn slavery alone is the easy way out, as trivial as Pierre Menard's first attempt to become Cervantes. What needs to be denounced here to restore authenticity is much less slavery than the racist present within which representations of slavery are produced. The moral incongruence stems from this uneasy overlap of the two sides of historicity.

Not surprisingly, survivors of all kinds are more likely than historians to denounce these trivializations. Thus, Vidal-Naquet warns us that if Holocaust narratives, even if empirically correct, lose their relationship to the living present, Jews and perhaps non-Jews would have suffered a moral defeat, and Holocaust survivors would have been returned symbolically to the camps. Pierre Weill approves in different terms: There is no purpose to the speeches and banners that marked the fiftieth celebration of Auschwitz's liberation by Soviet troops. The celebrations were a vain effort by state officials throughout the West to commemorate an impossible anniversary.

Survivors carry history on themselves, as Vidal-Naquet well knows. Indeed, a key difference between U.S. slavery and the European Holocaust is that no former slaves are alive today in the United States. This physical embodiment, a historical relation carried on the self, is crucial to Vidal-Naquet's distinction between history and memory. Thus, Vidal-Naquet worries about representations of the Holocaust once his generation is gone. But we should be careful not to push too far the distinction between various kinds of survivors. Weill, indeed, refuses to do so: As long as every living Jew, "regardless of age," remains an Auschwitz survivor, one cannot celebrate the liberation of Auschwitz.[8]

We are back into this present that we thought we could escape after the death of the last man.[9] It is from within this present that survivors, actors, and fellow narrators are asking us: what for? The meaning of history is also in its purpose. Empirical exactitude as defined and verified in specific context is necessary to historical production. But empirical exactitude alone is not enough. Historical representations—be they books, commercial exhibits or public commemorations—cannot be conceived only as vehicles for the transmission of knowledge. They must establish some relation to that knowledge. Further, not any relation will do. Authenticity is required, lest the representation becomes a fake, a morally repugnant spectacle.

By authenticity, I do not mean a mere simulacrum, a remake of Columbus's caravels, a mock battle on an anniversary or an exact model of a slave plantation. Neither do I mean a plunge into The Past. For how far can we plunge without trying to become Miguel de Cervantes in the way that Ménard first tried and found cheap and too easy? To be sure, injustices made to previous generations should be redressed: they affect the descendants of the victims. But the focus on The Past often diverts us from the present injustices for which previous generations only set the foundations.

From that viewpoint, the collective guilt of some white liberals toward "the slave past" of the United States, or the "colonial past" of Europe can be both misplaced and inauthentic. As a response to current accusations, it is misplaced inasmuch as these individuals are not responsible for the actions of their chosen ancestors. As a self-inflicted wound, it is comfortable inasmuch as it protects *them* from a racist present.

Indeed, none of us today can be true to Afro-American slavery—whether for or against it—as we can be true to ongoing practices of discrimination. Similarly, individuals in the Old World or in Latin America today cannot be true or false to a colonialism they did not live. What we know about slavery or about colonialism can—should, indeed—increase our ardor in the struggles against discrimination and oppression across racial and national boundaries. But no amount of historical research about the Holocaust and no amount of guilt about Germany's past can serve as a substitute for marching in the streets against German skinheads today. Fortunately, quite a few prominent German historians understand that much.

Authenticity implies a relation with what is known that duplicates the two sides of historicity: it engages us both as actors and narrators. Thus, authenticity cannot reside in attitudes toward a discrete past kept alive through narratives. Whether it invokes, claims, or rejects The Past, authenticity obtains only in regard to current practices that engage us as witnesses, actors, and commentators—including practices of historical narration. That the foundations of such practices were set by our precursors with the added value of their respective power is an inherent effect of the historicity of the human condition: none of us starts with a clean slate. But the historicity of the human condition also requires that practices of power and domination be renewed. It is that renewal that should concern us most, even if in the name of our pasts. The so-called legacies of past horrors—slavery, colonialism, or the Holocaust—are possible only because of that renewal. And that renewal occurs only in the present. Thus, even in relation to The Past our authenticity resides in the struggles of our present. Only in that present can we be true or false to the past we choose to acknowledge.

If authenticity belongs to the present, academic historians—and quite a few philosophers—may have lured themselves into a corner. The traditions of the guild, reinforced by a positivist philosophy of history, forbid academic historians to position themselves regarding the present. A fetishism of the facts, premised on an antiquated model of the natural sciences, still dominates history and the other social sciences. It reinforces the view that any conscious positioning should be rejected as ideological. Thus, the historian's position is officially unmarked: it is that of the nonhistorical observer.

The effects of this stance can be quite ironic. Since historical controversies often revolve on relevance—and therefore, at least in part, on the positioning of the observer—academic historians tend to keep as far away as possible from the historical controversies that most move the public of the day. In the United States, a few have intervened in the historical debates that made news in the early 1990s: the alleged role of Jews as slave owners, the Holocaust, the Alamo, the Smithsonian exhibits on the American West and on Hiroshima, or the Virginia park project.[10] But many more qualified historians have kept public silence on these and similar issues. That silence even extends to debates about the national standards for history that academics seem to have abandoned to pundits and politicians.

To be sure, the distance between scholarly and public discourses in the United States is extreme when compared, for instance, with the situation in France or in Germany.[11] American scholars have largely abandoned the role of public intellectual to pundits and entertainers. But the U.S. extreme tells us something about the continuum to which it belongs. At the heart of the noninvolvement of U.S. historians is the guild's traditional attachment to the fixity of pastness.

Professional historians have made good use of the creation of the past as a distinct entity, a creation that paralleled the growth of their own practice.[12] That practice, in turn, reinforced the belief that made it possible. The more historians wrote about past worlds, the more The Past became real as a separate world. But as various crises of our times impinge upon identities thought to be long established or silent, we move closer to the era when professional historians will have to position themselves more clearly within the present, lest politicians, magnates, or ethnic leaders alone write history for them.

Such positions need not be fixed, nor should they imply the ideological manipulation of empirical evidence. Practicing historians who advocate a history aware of its purpose—from the presentists of the first half of this century to the leftists of the 1970s—never suggested such manipulation.[13] Most of these advocates, however, assumed the possibility of either an unambiguous narrative, or of an unambiguous present. With varying degrees of certitude, they envisioned that narratives about the past could expose with utmost clarity positions solidly anchored in the present. We now know that narratives are made of silences, not all of which are deliberate or even perceptible as such within the time of their production. We also know that the present is itself no clearer than the past.

None of these discoveries entails an absence of purpose. They certainly do not entail an abandonment of the search and defense of values that distinguish the intellectual from a mere scholar.[14] Positions need not be eternal in order to justify a legitimate defense. To miss this point is to bypass the historicity of the human condition. Any search for eternity condemns us to the impossible choice between fiction and positivist truth, between nihilism and fundamentalism, which are two sides of the same coin. As we move through the end of the millenium, it will be increasingly tempting to seek salvation by faith alone, now that most deeds seem to have failed.

But we may want to keep in mind that deeds and words are not as distinguishable as we often presume. History does not belong only to its narrators, professional or amateur. While some of us debate what history is or was, others take it in their own hands.

Epilogue

I was looking for Columbus, but I knew that he would not be there. Down by the shore, Port-au-Prince exposed its wounds to the sun; and Harry Truman Boulevard, once the most beautiful street of Haiti, was now a patchwork of potholes.

The boulevard was built for the bicentennial celebration of Port-au-Prince, which Truman helped finance right between his launching of the North Atlantic Treaty Organization and the start of the Korean War. Now, it looked like a war zone with no memory of the celebrations of which it had been the center. Only a few of the statues erected for the occasion remained. Its fountains had dried up under two Duvaliers. Its palm trees had shrunk as had Haiti itself.

I turned in front of the French Institute, a living monument to the impact of French culture on the Haitian elites, and drove toward the U.S. embassy, a center of power of a different order. Above a mountain of sandbags, a helmeted black G.I. watched nonchalantly as a crowd of half-naked boys bathed in a puddle left by yesterday's rain. He had probably come with the occupying forces that helped restore President Jean-Bertrand Aristide to power in 1994. The story I was looking for went back to nine years earlier. I drove by.

I stopped the car at safe enough distance from the embassy and started a slow walk on the boulevard. On the buildings around the post office, conflicting graffittis asked the U.S. forces both to stay and to go home. I spotted a statue lying behind a fence across the street. A peddling artist stood next to it, selling paintings and crafts. I greeted the man and asked him if he knew where the statue of Christopher Columbus was.

I had vague memories of that statue. I only remembered its existence from my adolescent wanderings. The few images I could summon came from Graham Greene's "The Comedians." It was under the watchful eyes of Columbus that the heroes of that story, later played by Richard Burton and Elizabeth Taylor, consummated their illicit love. But the bust on the grass was no Columbus. The painter confirmed my doubts. "No," he said, "this is a statue of Charlemagne Péralte."

Péralte was the leader of a nationalist army that fought the first occupation of Haiti by the United States in the 1920s. From the pictures the Marines took of him after they had crucified him on a door, I knew that he was a thin dark man. The bust on the grass was visibly that of a white male, rather stocky. "You're sure this is Péralte?" I asked again. "Sure is Péralte," replied the painter. I moved closer and read the inscription. The sculpture was a bust of Harry Truman.

"Where is the Columbus one?" I asked.

"I don't know. I am not from Port-au-Prince," replied the man. "Maybe it is the one that used to be near the water."

I walked to the place he indicated. No statue was to be found. The pedestal was still there, but the sculpture itself was missing. Someone had inscribed on the cement: "Charlemagne Péralte Plaza." Truman had become Péralte and Péralte had replaced Columbus.

I stood there for another half hour, asking each passerby if they knew what had happened to the Columbus statue. I knew the story: I was in Port-au-Prince when Columbus disappeared. I just wanted confirmation, a test of how public memory works and how history takes shape in a country with the lowest literacy rate on this side of the Atlantic.

I was almost ready to give up when a young man recapped for me the events I had first heard about in 1986. In that year, at the fall of Jean-Claude Duvalier's dictatorship, the most miserable people of Haiti's capital had taken to the streets. They had thrown their anger at every monument that they associated with the dictatorship. A number of statues had been broken into pieces; others were simply removed from their bases. This was how Truman came to find himself on the grass.

Columbus had a different fate, for reasons still unknown to me. Perhaps the illiterate demonstrators associated his name with colonialism. The mistake, if mistake there was, is understandable: the word "kolon" in Haitian means both Columbus and a colonist. Perhaps they associated him with the ocean from which he came. At any rate, when the angry crowd from the neighboring shanty towns rolled down the Harry Truman Boulevard, they took the statue of Columbus, removed it from its pedestal, and dumped it into the sea.

Notes

1 The Power of the Story

1 Theories of history that have generated so many debates, models, and schools of thought since at least the early nineteenth century have been the object of a number of studies, anthologies, and summaries. See Henri-Irénée Marrou, *De la Connaissance historique* (Paris: Seuil, 1975 [1954]); Patrick Gardiner, ed., *The Philosophy of History* (Oxford: Oxford University Press, 1974); William Dray, *On History and Philosophers of History* (Leiden, New York: Brill, 1989); Robert Novick, *That Noble Dream: The "Objectivity Question" and the American Historical Profession* (Cambridge: Cambridge University Press, 1988). My trust here is that too many conceptualizations of history tend to privilege one side of historicity over the other; that most debates about the nature of history, in turn, spring from one or another version of this one-sidedness; and that this one-sidedness itself is possible because most theories of history are built without much attention to the process of production of specific historical narratives.

Many writers have tried to chart a course between the two poles described here. A number of broken lines from the Marx of *Eighteenth Brumaire*, to the work of Jean Chesnaux, Marc Ferro, Michel de Certeau, David W. Cohen, Ranajit Guha, Krzysztof Pomian, Adam Schaff, and Tzvetan Todorov crisscross this book, not always through the mechanical means of citations. See Jean Chesneaux, *Du Passé faisons table rase* (Paris: F. Maspero, 1976); David W. Cohen, *The Combing of History* (Chicago: University of Chicago Press, 1994); Michel de Certeau, *L'Écriture de l'histoire* (Paris: Gallimard, 1975); Marc Ferro, *L'Histoire sous surveillance* (Paris: Calmann-Lévy, 1985); Ranajit Guha, "The Prose of Counter Insurgency," *Subaltern Studies*, vol. 2, 1983; Karl Marx, *The Eighteenth Brumaire of Louis Bonaparte* (London: G. Allen & Unwin, 1926); Krzysztof Pomian, *L'Ordre du temps* (Paris: Gallimard, 1984); Adam Schaff, *History and Truth* (Oxford: Pergamon

Press, 1976); Tzvetan Todorov, *Les Morales de l'histoire* (Paris: Bernard Grasset, 1991).

2 Todorov, *les Morales*, 129–130.

3 Hayden White, *Metahistory: The Historical Imagination in Nineteenth-Century Europe* (Baltimore: The Johns Hopkins University Press, 1973); *Tropics of Discourse: Essays in Cultural Criticism* (Baltimore: The Johns Hopkins University Press, 1978); *The Content of the Form: Narrative Discourse and Historic Representation* (Baltimore: The Johns Hopkins University Press, 1987).

4 In fact, each narrative must renew this claim twice. From the viewpoint of its immediate producer(s), the narrative makes a claim to knowledge: that which is said to have happened is said to be known to have happened. Every historian delivers a narrative with a certificate of authenticity, however qualified. From the viewpoint of its audience, the historical narrative must pass a test of acceptance, which reinforces the claim to knowledge: that which is said to have happened is believed to have happened.

5 See Todorov, *Les Morales*, 130–169, for a discussion of the differences between fiction, fake, and historical writing and on various kinds of truth claims. See also chap. 5, below, on authenticity.

6 Pomian, *L'Ordre du temps*, 109–111.

7 Evidentials are grammaticalized constructions through which speakers express their commitment to a proposition in light of the available evidence. See David Crystal, *A Dictionary of Linguistics and Phonetics*, 3d ed. (Oxford: Basil Blackwell, 1991), 127. For example, the difference in epistemic modality between a witness and a non-witness could be a grammaticalized requirement.

8 Arjun Appadurai, "The Past as a Scarce Resource," *Man* 16 (1981): 201–219.

9 For updates on that discussion, see Paula Brown and Donald F. Tuzin, editors, *The Ethnography of Cannibalism* (Washington, D.C.: Society for Psychological Anthropology, 1983); Peter Hulme, *Colonial Encounters* (London and New York: Methuen, 1986); and Philip P. Boucher, *Cannibal Encounters* (Baltimore: The Johns Hopkins University Press, 1992).

10 Ralph W. Steen, *Texas: A Story of Progress* (Austin: Steck, 1942), 182; Adrian N. Anderson and Ralph Wooster, *Texas and Texans* (Austin: Steck-Vaughn, 1978), 171.

11 This partial list of disputed "facts" and my understanding of the Alamo controversy are based on oral and written sources. Research assistant Rebecca Bennette conducted phone interviews with Gail Loving Barnes of the Daughters of the Republic of Texas and Gary J. (Gabe) Gabehart of the Inter-Tribal Council. Thanks to both of them, as well as Carlos Guerra, for their cooperation. Written sources include articles in local newspapers (especially the *San Antonio Express News*, which publishes Guerra's column): Carlos Guerra, "Is Booty Hidden Near the Alamo?" *San Antonio Light*, 22 August 1992; Carlos Guerra, "You'd Think All Alamo Saviors Look Alike," *San Antonio Express News*, 14 February 1994; and Robert Rivard, "The Growing Debate Over the Shrine of Texas Liberty," *San Antonio Express News*, 17 March 1994. They include also academic journals: Edward Tabor Linenthal, "A Reservoir of Spiritual Power: Patriotic Faith at the Alamo in the Twentieth Century," *Southwestern Historical Quarterly* 91 (4) (1988): 509–31; Stephen L. Hardin, "The Félix Nuñez Account and the Siege of the Alamo: A Critical Appraisal," *Southwestern Historical Quarterly* 94 (1990): 65–84; as well as the controversial book—Jeff Long, *Duel of Eagles: The Mexican and the U.S. Fight for the Alamo* (New York: William Morrow, 1990).

12 Arthur A. Butz, "The International 'Holocaust' Controversy," *The Journal of Historical Review* (n.d.): 5–20; Robert Faurisson, "The Problem of the Gas Chambers," *Journal of Historical Review* (1980).

13 Pierre Vidal-Naquet, *Les Assassins de la mémoire: "Un Eichmann de papier" et Autres essais sur le révisionnisme* (Paris: La Découverte, 1987); Jean-Claude Pressac, *Les Crématoires d'Auschwitz: La machinerie de meurtre de masse* (Paris: CNRS, 1993); Deborah E. Lipstadt, *Denying the Holocaust: The Growing Assault on Truth and Memory* (New York: The Free Press, 1993); Faurisson, "The Problem of the Gas Chambers"; Mark Weber, "A Prominent Historian Wrestles with a Rising Revisionism," *Journal of Historical Review* 11 (3) (1991): 353–359.

The differences between these rebuttals offer lessons in historical strategies. Pressac's book faces head-on the revisionist's challenge to treat the Holocaust as any other historical controversy and to deal with the facts and just the facts. It is the most "academic" in an old-fashioned way. Almost three-hundred footnotes of archival references, numerous pictures, graphs, and tables document the massive death machinery set up by the Nazis. Lipstadt takes the position that there should be no debate on "facts," because such debate legitimizes revisionism; but she engages the revisionists polemically on their political motivations, which seems to me no less legitimizing and requires numerous allusions to empirical controversies. Vidal-Naquet consciously rejects the proposition that debates on "facts" and ideology are mutually exclusive. Although he avoids name-calling, he continuously expresses his moral outrage not only at the revisionist narrative but at the Holocaust. There would be no revisionism if there was no Holocaust. This strategy leaves him room for both a methodological and political critique of revisionism, and for empirical challenge on the "facts" he chooses to debate. Vidal-Naquet also avoids the trap of Jewish exceptionalism, which could easily lead to a view of history as revenge and justify use and misuse of the Holocaust narrative: Auschwitz cannot explain Chabra and Chatila.

14 As noted, there are wide variations in the views expressed by the revisionists, but the last fifteen years have seen a shift toward a more academic stance, to which I shall return.

15 White, *The Content of Form.*

16 See Hayden White, "Historical Emplotment and the Problem of Truth," in *Probing the Limits of Representation*, S. Friendlander, ed., (Berkeley: University of California Press, 1992), 37–53.

17 H. Ebbinghaus, *Memory: A Contribution to Experimental Psychology* (New York: Dover, 1964 [1885]); A. J. Cascardi, "Remembering," *Review of Metaphysics* 38 (1984): 275–302; Henry L. Roediger, "Implicit Memory: Retention Without Remembering," *American Psychologist* 45 (1990): 1043–1056; Robin Green and David Shanks, "On the Existence of Independent Explicit and Implicit Learning Systems: An Examination of Some Evidence," *Memory and Cognition* 21 (1993): 304–317; D. Broadbent, "Implicit and Explicit Knowledge in the Control of Complex Systems," *British Journal of Psychology* 77 (1986): 33–50; Daniel L. Schackter, "Understanding Memory: A Cognitive Neuroscience Approach," *American Psychologist* 47 (1992): 559–569; Elizabeth Loftus, "The Reality of Repressed Memories," *American Psychologist* 48 (1993): 518–537.

18 U.S. figures do not include the colony of Lousiana. For the narrative and sources behind these estimates, see Philip Curtin, *The Atlantic Slave Trade: A Census* (Madison: University of Wisconsin Press, 1969). Partial updates of Curtin's figures on exports from Africa do not invalidate the general picture he provides for imports throughout the Americas.

19 Robert William Fogel and Stanley L. Engerman, *Time on the Cross: The Economics of American Negro Slavery* (Boston: Little, Brown, 1974); B. W. Higman, *Slave Populations of the British Caribbean, 1807–1834* (Baltimore: The Johns Hopkins University Press, 1984); Ira Berlin and Philip D. Morgan, eds., *Cultivation and Culture: Labor and the Shaping of Life in the Americas* (Charlottesville: The University Press of Virginia, 1993); Robert William Fogel, *Without Consent or Contract: The Rise and Fall of American Slavery* (New York: W. W. Norton, 1989).

20 W. E. B. Du Bois, *Some Efforts of American Negroes for Their Own Social Betterment* (Atlanta: The Atlanta University Press, 1898); *Black Reconstruction in America: An Essay Toward a History of the Part Which Black Folk Played in the At-*

tempt to Reconstruct Democracy in America, 1860–1880 (New York: Russell and Russell, 1962); Eric Foner, *Reconstruction: America's Unfinished Revolution, 1863–1877* (New York: Harper & Row, 1988).

21 E.g., Du Bois, *Black Reconstruction*; Edward Franklin Frazier, *Black Bourgeoisie* (Glencoe: Free Press, 1957); Melville J. Herskovits, *The Myth of the Negro Past* (Boston: Beacon Press, 1990 [1941]); Gunnar Myrdal, *An American Dilemma: The Negro Problem and Modern Democracy* (New York, London: Harper & Bros. 1944).

22 Paul Ricoeur rightly notes that both the logical positivists and their adversaries launched and sustained their long debate on the nature of historical knowledge with little attention to the actual practice of historians. Paul Ricoeur, *Time and Narrative*, vol. 1, trans. Kathleen Mclaughlin and David Pellauer (Chicago: University of Chicago Press, 1984), 95. Ricoeur himself uses abundantly the work of academic historians from Europe and the United States. Other recent writers also make use of past and current historical works, with various degrees of emphasis on particular schools or countries, and with various digressions on the relationship between the development of history and that of other institutionalized forms of knowledge. See De Certeau, *L'Écriture*; François Furet, *L'Atelier de l'histoire* (Paris: Flammarion, 1982); Joyce Appleby, Lynn Hunt, and Margaret Jacob, *Telling the Truth about History* (New York: W. W. Norton, 1994). Such works bring theory closer to the observation of actual practice, but is historical production limited to the practice of professional historians? First, from a phenomenologist's viewpoint, one could argue that all human beings have a pre-thematic awareness of history that functions as background for their experience of the social process. See David Carr, *Time, Narrative, and History* (Bloomington: Indiana University Press, 1986), 3. Second, and more important for our purposes here, narrative history itself is not produced only by professional historians. See Cohen, *The Combing of History*; Ferro, *L'Histoire sous surveillance*; Paul Thompson, *The Myths We Live By* (London and New York: Routledge, 1990).

23 Ferro, *L'Histoire sous surveillance.*

24 Dorothy Ross, *The Origins of American Social Science* (Cambridge and New York: Cambridge University Press, 1994).

25 Crocket himself contributed to his perception as hero, starting with his autobiography. But his historical significance remained limited until the television series and John Wayne's 1960 movie, *The Alamo*, made him a national figure.

26 Remarkable exceptions, each in its own way, are Cohen's *The Combing*, Ferro's *L'Histoire sous surveillance*, and de Certeau's *L'Écriture de l'histoire.*

27 Indeed, most of the times that the word "history" will be used henceforth, it will be used primarily with that meaning in mind. I reserve the words sociohistorical process for the other part of the distinction.

28 I label the occupants of such and other structural positions *agents* to indicate at the onset a rejection of the structure/agency dichotomy. Structural positions are both enabling and limiting.

29 See Alain Touraine, *Le Retour de l'acteur* (Paris: Gallimard, 1984), 14–15.

30 I expand here on W. G. Runciman, *A Treatise on Social Theory*, vol. I: *The Methodology of Social Theory* (Cambridge: Cambridge University Press, 1983), 31–34.

31 Ferro, *L'Histoire sous surveillance*; Marshall Sahlins, *Historical Metaphors and Mythical Realities: Structure in Early History of the Sandwich Islands Kingdom* (Ann Arbor: University of Michigan Press, 1981); Hélène Carrère d'Encausse, *La Gloire des nations, ou, la fin de l'empire soviétique* (Paris: Fayard, 1990); Francis Fukuyama, *The End of History and the Last Man* (New York: Free Press, 1992); William F. Lewis, "Telling America's Story: Narrative Form and the Reagan Presidency," *Quarterly Journal of Speech* 73 (1987): 280–302.

32 Michel Foucault, "On Power" (original interview with Pierre Boncenne, 1978) in Michel Foucault, *Politics, Philosophy, Culture. Interviews and Other Writings*, ed. Lawrence D. Kritzman (New York and London: Routledge, 1988), 103.

33 Oral history does not escape that law, except that in the case of oral transmission, the moment of fact creation is continually carried over in the very bodies of the individuals who partake in that transmission. The *source* is alive.

2 The Three Faces of Sans Souci

1 I have not done fieldwork on the oral history of Sans Souci. I suspect that there is much more in the oral archives than this summary, which encapsulates only "popular" knowledge in the area as filtered through the routine performances of the guides.

2 Karl Ritter, *Naturhistorische Reise nach der westindischen Insel Hayti* (Stuttgart: Hallberger'fche Berlagshandlung, 1836), 77; John Candler, *Brief Notices of Haiti: with its Conditions, Resources, and Prospects* (London: Thames Ward, 1842); Jonathan Brown, *The History and Present Condition of St. Domingo* (Philadelphia: W. Marshall, 1837), 186; Prince Sanders, ed., *Haytian Papers. A Collection of the Very Interesting Proclamations* (London: Printed for W. Reed, 1816); Aimé Césaire, *La Tragédie du roi Christophe* (Paris: Présence Africaine, 1963); Alejo Carpentier, *The Kingdom of This World* (New York: Alfred A. Knopf, 1983 [1949]); Pompée Valentin Baron de Vastey, *An Essay on the Causes of the Revolution and Civil Wars of Hayti* (Exeter: printed at the Western Luminary Office, 1923 [1819]), 137.

3 Cited in Thomas Madiou, *Histoire d'Haïti*, tome II: 1799–1803 (Port-au-Prince: Editions Henri Deschamps, 1989 [1847]), 172–73.

4 Jean Baptiste Romain identifies a coffee area named Sans Souci in colonial times between what is now Vallières and Mombin-Crochu, more than forty kilometers southeast of Milot. Currently, Sans Souci refers not only to the Milot palace, but also to a rural area of a few hundred inhabitants, around Bois Laurence in the commune of Mombin. Jean-Baptiste Romain, *Noms de lieux d'époque coloniale en Haïti. Essai sur la toponymie du Nord à l'usage des étudiants* (Port-au-Prince: Imprimerie de l'État, 1960).

5 Gros, *Récit historique sur les évènements* (Paris: De l'Imprimerie Parent, 1793), 12–14.

6 John K. Thornton, "African Soldiers in the Haitian Revolution," *The Journal of Caribbean History* 25, nos. 1, 2 (1991): 58–80.

7 Claude B. Auguste and Marcel B. Auguste, *L'expédition Leclerc, 1801–1803* (Port-au-Prince: Imprimerie Henri Deschamps, 1986), 189. Italics mine. There was a long-standing animosity between Christophe and Sans Souci, the cause of which remains unknown. The French intended to make full use of this personal conflict to set Christophe against Sans Souci; but Christophe disappointed them, showing little enthusiasm in this first campaign. See François Joseph Pamphile, Vicomte de Lacroix, *Mémoires pour servir à l'histoire de la révolution de Saint-Domingue*, 2 vols. (Paris: Pillet Ainé, 1819), 220–221.

8 Auguste and Auguste, *L'expédition Leclerc*, 188–198.

9 French general Pamphile de Lacroix, a veteran of the Saint-Domingue expedition, later noted in his memoirs his surprise at Sans Souci's military effectiveness. Christophe himself came close to suggesting that if the colonial troops had used guerilla tactics similar to those of Sans Souci they would not have lost the first phase of the war against the French. Lacroix, *Mémoires*, 219, 228.

10 Laura V. Monti, *A Calendar of the Rochambeau Papers of the University of Florida Libraries* (Gainesville: University of Florida Libraries, 1972).

11 To claim otherwise would be to suggest that a "source" can be "the thing" itself, which is nonsense. Because facts are not "things" (they cannot be asserted only—if at all—on ontologial grounds), sources are always *about* something else.

12 Even scholars who can hardly be accused of empiricism sometimes come close to equating a "new" history with a turn toward new objects defined in terms of their content-matter. See Jacques Le Goff and P. Nora, eds., *Faire de l'histoire,* vols. 2, 3 (Paris: Gallimard, 1974). To be fair to Le Goff, Nora et al., most French historians have learned since the 1950s that the historical subject is constructed. That was, in retrospect, the epistemological lesson of the historians associated with the French historical journal, *Annales.* That the turn to new objects was translated by many in the Anglo-Saxon tradition as an empirical discovery is nevertheless telling.

13 E.g., Krzysztof Pomian, *L'Ordre du temps* (Paris: Gallimard, 1984); David Carr, *Time, Narrative and History* (Bloomington: Indiana University Press, 1986).

14 W. H. Dray, "Narration, Reduction and the Uses of History," in David Carr, William Dray, Theodore Geraets, *La Philosophie de l'histoire et la pratique historienne d'aujourd'hui/Philosophy of History and Contemporary Histiography* (Ottawa: University of Ottawa Press, 1982), 203. This distinction is similar to that between description and narration. I am not very keen on either of these divisions when phrased in terms of contents, or even in terms of organization. A list without a point is not an easy one to make. I admit, however, an irreducible distance between the viewpoint of the chronicler as witness and actor, and the viewpoint of the narrator as storybuilder. That distance reflects the ambiguous mix of the two sides of historicity. Second, the distinction in terms of viewpoints allow us to distinguish between narrator and author as potentially different voices (Pomian, *L'Ordre du Temps*). For a critique of the possibility of an ideal chronicler, see Paul Roth, "Narrative Explanations: The Case of History," *History and Theory* XXVII (1988): 1–13, and pp. 51, 55 below.

15 B. W. Higman, *Slave Populations of the British Caribbean,* 1807–1834 (Baltimore: The Johns Hopkins University Press, 1984).

16 Emile Benveniste, *Le Vocabulaire des institutions indo-européenes* (Paris: Minuit, 1969), 143.

17 Michel de Certeau, *L'Écriture de l'histoire* (Paris: Gallimard, 1975), 20–21.

18 The difference duplicates somewhat that of the viewpoint between chronicler and narrator. While sources remain close to the material traces of participation, archives already condition facts toward narratives.

19 The history of the Rochambeau Papers is itself an archival story full of silences. They were brought by the University of Florida from Sotheby, but how they came to Sotheby remains a mystery: there is no record of provenance (Monti, *Rochambeau Papers*, 4). Some Haitians suggest that the appropriation of the papers by whomever Sotheby was acting for could very well be a case study of the quite concrete effects of differential power in the international market for documents.

20 E.g., Gros, *Récit historique*; de Lacroix, *Mémoires*; Beaubrun Ardouin, *Études sur l'histoire d'Haïti* (Port-au-Prince: François Dalencourt, 1958); Hubert Cole, *Christophe, King of Haïti* (New York: Viking, 1967); Jacques Thibau, *Le Temps de Saint-Domingue: L'esclavage et la révolution française* (Paris: J. C. Lattes, 1989).

21 At one point during the war within the war, he told the French that he would surrender only if they expelled Christophe, a proposition a French witness refers to as a "pretext." de Lacroix, *Mémoires*, 220.

22 Monti, *Rochambeau Papers*.

23 Auguste and Auguste, *L'expédition Leclerc*.

24 Michel-Rolph Trouillot, *Ti difé boulé sou istoua Ayiti* (New York: Koleksion Lakansièl, 1977).

25 Hénock Trouillot, *Le gouvernement du Roi Henri Christophe* (Port-au-Prince: Imprimerie Centrale, 1972), 29.

26 There are, in this story, a number of telling silences, both collective and individual, the motives for which we can only guess, both doubtful and genuine. William Harvey, of Queens College (Cambridge), who served as Christophe's adviser during months of residence in Haiti and wrote what may pass for the King's first biography, flatly states that the palace was named "probably, from the manner in which it was defended by nature." See W. W. Harvey, *Sketches of Hayti; from the Expulsion of the French to the Death of Christophe* (London: L. B. Seeley and Son, 1827), 133. Whether Harvey, who moved extensively within the kingdom, heard either about the Colonel or Potsdam is not clear. But he had the prudence that has come to characterize foreign consultants, and "nature" may have looked to him as a perfect alibi. Similarly, one can tie the silence of some Haitian witnesses, such as de Vastey, to a desire to preserve a favorable image of Christophe.

27 Lacroix, *Mémoires*, 227, 287. The conversation mentioned, which occurred in the first phase of the war within the war, already suggests Christophe's wish to make of Sans Souci a non-object of discourse. In the course of the exchange, de

Lacroix bluntly challenged Christophe's claims to fame, hinting that if Christophe was as popular and respected as he affirmed he would have convinced the blacks to betray Sans Souci. (Note the pattern of induced betrayal.) As the French general later reports the exchange, Christophe dodged the issue of command and popularity. He called Sans Souci a "brigand," displacing into the field of Western tastefulness what was a serious competition for national leadership.

28 Jonathan Brown, *The History and Present Condition of St. Domingo*, vol. 2 (Philadelphia: W. Marshall, 1837), 216.

29 Hérard Dumesle, *Voyage dans le Nord d'Hayti* (Cayes: Imprimerie du gouvernement, 1824), 225–226.

30 Vergniaud Leconte, *Henri Christophe dans l'histoire d'Haïti* (Paris: Berger-Levrault, 1931), 273.

31 Harvey, *Sketches of Hayti.*

32 Charles Mackenzie, *Notes on Haiti, Made During a Residence in that Republic*, vol. 2 (London: Henry Colburn and Richard Bentley, 1830), 209; *Notes on Haiti*, vol. 1, 169–179.

33 Ritter, *Insel Hayti*, 77, 78, 81.

34 Ibid., 76.

35 Ibid., 77–82.

36 Cole, *Christophe*, 207.

37 For the record, Cole was often sympathetic to his subject. My point is that this sympathy pertains to a particular field of significance that characterizes treatments of the Haitian Revolution by Western historians. See chap. 3.

38 René Phelipeau, *Plan de la plaine du Cap François en l'isle Saint Domingue* (hand copy, Bibliothèque Nationale, Paris, 1786).

39 Possible corroboration of this interpretation is an ephemeral change in the name of Grand Pré itself. Sometime between the death of Sans Souci and 1827, the plantation was rebaptized "La Victoire" (The Victory). Mackenzie's first volume opens with a picture of a plantation "La Victoire, formerly Grand Pré, on the road to Sans Souci (Mackenzie, *Notes on Haiti*, vol. 1., frontispiece). Unfortunately, we do not know if the name change occurred during Christophe's tenure or in the seven years between his death and Mackenzie's visit.

40 Robert Norris, *Memoirs of the Reign of Bossa Adahee, King of Dahomy* (London: Frank Cass, 1968 [1789]), xiv. On "mulatto" historians and the Haitian past, see David Nicholls, *From Dessalines to Duvalier: Race, Colour and National Independence in Haiti*, chap. 3 (London: MacMillan Caribbean, 1988). On Ardouin in particular, see Hénock Trouillot, *Beaubrun Ardouin, l'homme politique et l'historien* (Mexico: Instituto Panamericano de Geografía e Historia, Comision de Historia, 1950). For a close reading of Ardouin, see Drexel G. Woodson, "Tout mounn se mounn men tout mounn pa menm: Microlevel Sociocultural Aspects of Land Tenure in a Northern Haitian Locality" (Ph.D. diss., University of Chicago, 1990). On class and color in Haiti, see Michel-Rolph Trouillot, *Haiti: State against Nation* (New York and London: Monthly Review Press, 1989).

41 Lacroix, *Mémoires*, vol. 2, 287; Leconte, *Henri Christophe*, 282.

42 Thornton, "African Soldiers in the Haitian Revolution."

43 Auguste and Auguste, *L'Expédition Leclerc.*

44 Ardouin, *Études sur l'histoire d'Haiti*, vol. 5, 75.

45 On elites' appropriation and control of mass aspirations in postcolonial state building, see Trouillot, *Ti dife boule*; Trouillot, *Haiti: State against Nation.* For a model study of these issues in India and Indian historiography, see Partha Chatterjee, *The Nation and its Fragments: Colonial and Postcolonial Histories* (Princeton: Princeton University Press, 1993).

3 An Unthinkable History

1 Quoted by Roger Dorsinville in *Toussaint Louverture ou La vocation de la Liberté* (Paris: Julliard, 1965).

2 Cited by Jacques Cauna in *Au temps des isles à sucre* (Paris: Karthala, 1987), 204.

3 Most of these pamphlets, including those cited here, are included in the Lk12 series at the Bibliothèque Nationale, in Paris. Others were reproduced by the French government (e.g., French National Assembly, *Pièces imprimées par ordre de l'Assemblée Nationale, Colonies* (Paris: Imprimerie Nationale, 1791–92).

4 Michel-Rolph Trouillot, "Anthropology and the Savage Slot: The Poetics and Politics of Otherness," in *Recapturing Anthropology: Working in the Present*, ed. Richard G. Fox (Santa Fe: School of American Research Press, 1991), 17–44.

5 Michael Adas, *Machines as the Measure of Men: Science, Technology and Ideologies of Western Domination*, chap. 2 (Ithaca: Cornell University Press, 1989). Psalmanazar's hoax about cannibalism in Taiwan captivated interest in Europe between 1704 and 1764 exactly because it played on these preconceptions. See Tzvetan Todorov, *Les Morales de l'histoire* (Paris: Bernard Grasset, 1991), 134–141. For an earlier example of admiration and contempt for the Orient, see John Chardin's *Travels*, in which the Persians are "Dissemblers, Cheats and the basest and most impudent Flattereres in the World" and, two pages later, "the most Civiliz'd People of the East," 187–189. John Chardin, *Travels in Persia 1673–1677* (New York: Dover, 1988; originally published in Amsterdam, 1711).

6 *Notre Librairie* (October–December 1987) no. 90, Images du noir dans la littérature occidentale; vol. I: Du Moyen-Age à la conquête coloniale. Simone Delesalle and Lucette Valensi, "Le mot 'nègre' dans les dictionnaires français d'ancien régime: histoire et lexicographie," *Langues françaises*, no. 15.

7 Gordon Lewis, *Main Currents in Caribbean Thoughts, The Historical Evolution of Caribbean Society in its Ideological Aspects, 1492–1900,* chap. 3 (Baltimore: The Johns Hopkins University Press, 1983); William B. Cohen, *The French Encounter with Africans: White Response to Blacks, 1530–1880* (Bloomington: Indiana University Press, 1980); Winthrop D. Jordan, *White over Black: American Attitudes toward the Negro, 1550–1812* (Chapel Hill: University of North Carolina Press, 1968); Serge Daget, "Le mot esclave, nègre et noir et les jugements de valeur sur la traite négrière dans la littérature abolitioniste française de 1770 à 1845," *Revue française d'histoire d'outre-mer* 60, no. 4 (1973): 511–48; Pierre Boulle, "In Defense of Slavery: Eighteenth-Century Opposition to Abolition and the Origins of Racist Ideology in France," in *History from Below: Studies in Popular Protest and Popular Ideology*, ed. Frederick Krantz (London: Basil Blackwell, 1988), 219–246. Louis Sala-Molins, *Misères des Lumières. Sous la raison, l'outrage* (Paris: Robert Laffont, 1992); Michèle Duchet, "Au temps des philosophes," *Notre Librairie* (October–December 1987) no. 90, Images du noir, 25–33.

8 *Archives Parlementaires*, 1st ser. vol. 8 (session of 3 July 1789), 186.

9 Tzvetan Todorov, *The Deflection of the Enlightenment* (Stanford: Stanford Humanities Center, 1989), 4.

10 Jacques Thibau, *Le Temps de Saint-Domingue. L'esclavage et la révolution française* (Paris: Jean-Claude Lattès, 1989), 92.

11 Michèle Duchet, *Anthropologie et histoire au siècle des Lumières* (Paris: Maspero, 1971), 157. Emphasis added. On anticolonialism in France, see Yves Benot, *La Révolution française et la fin des colonies* (Paris: La Découverte, 1987); *La Démence coloniale sous Napoléon* (Paris: La Découverte, 1992).

12 David Geggus, "Racial Equality, Slavery, and Colonial Secession during the Constituent Assembly," *American Historical Review* 94, no. 5 (December 1989): 1290–1308; Daget, "Le mot esclave"; Sala-Molins, *Misères.*

13 Raynald, Guillaume-François, *Histoire des deux Indes*, 7 vols. (The Hague: Grosse, 1774). Michèle Duchet, *Diderot et l'Histoire des deux Indes ou l'écriture fragmentaire* (Paris: Nizet, 1978); Yves Benot, *Diderot, de l'athéisme à l'anti-colonialisme* (Paris: Maspero, 1970), *La Révolution française.*

14 Duchet, *Diderot et l'Histoire*; Michel Delon 'L'Appel au lecteur dans l'Histoire des deux Indes," in *Lectures de Raynal. L'Histoire des deux Indes en Europe et en Amérique au XVIIIe siècle*, (eds.) Hans-Jürgen Lüsebrink and Manfred Tietz (Oxford: Voltaire Foundation, 1991), 53–66; Yves Benot, "Traces de l'*Histoire des deux Indes* chez les anti-esclavagistes sous la Révolution," in *Lectures de Raynal*, 141–154.

15 Jean-Claude Bonnet. *Diderot. Textes et débats* (Paris: Livre de Poche, 1984), 416. On the construction of European civilization implicit in the *Histoire*, see Gabrijela Vidan, "Une reception fragmentée: le cas de Raynal en terres slaves du Sud," in *Lectures de Raynal*, 361–372.

16 Louis Sala-Molins, *Le Code noir ou le calvaire de Canaan* (Paris: PUF, Pratiques Théoriques, 1987), 254–261. In Benot's apt phrase, autonomy was "fatally white" whenever it came up in the *Histoire* (Benot, "Traces de *l'Histoire*," 147).

17 Serge Daget, "Le mot esclave, nègre et noir," 519.

18 Yves Benot, *Diderot*, 316. Emphasis added.

19 Pierre Bourdieu, *Le Sens pratique* (Paris: Minuit, 1980), 14. The unthinkable applies to the world of everyday life and to the social sciences. See *Le Sens pratique*, 90, 184, 224, 272.

20 There is no term in the vocabulary of the times either in English or in French that would account for the practices—or encapsulate a generalized notion—of resistance. I use resistance here in the rather loose way it appears nowadays in the literature. I am dealing elsewhere with the necessary distinction between resistance and defiance and the concept of resistance. Michel-Rolph Trouillot, "In the Shadow of the West: Power, Resistance and Creolization in the Caribbean." Keynote lecture at the Congress, "Born out of Resistance," Afro-Caribische Culturen, Center for Caribbean and Latin American Studies, Risjksuniversiteit Utrecht, Netherlands, 26 March 1992.

21 "Nature has at last created this stunning man, this immortal man, who must deliver a world from the most atrocious, the longest, the most insulting tyranny. He has shattered the irons of his compatriots. So many oppressed slaves under the most odious slavery seemed to wait only for his signal to make such a hero. This heroic avenger has set an example that sooner or later cruelty will be punished, and that Providence holds in store these strong souls, which she releases upon earth to reestablish the equilibrium which the inequity of ferocious ambition knew how to destroy." (Mercier, *L'An 2440*, xxii, in Bonnet, *Diderot*, 331).

22 Whether Louverture himself had read Raynal in 1791 and was convinced of his own future role in history is unproven and beside the point.

23 In Benot, *Diderot*, 214; Duchet, *Anthropologie et histoire*, 175. Emphasis added.

24 Interpellation is one of the favorite tropes of the Enlightenment, abundantly used in the *Histoire* for a number of political and rhetorical reasons. Michel Delon, "L'Appel au lecteur."

25 "Ces fers dès longtemps préparés . . . pour nous . . . / C'est nous qu'on ose méditer / De rendre à l'antique esclavage" etc. (*La Marseillaise*).

26 *Archives Parlementaires*, vol. 9 (session of 22 October 1789), 476–478.

27 Lucien Jaume, *Les Déclarations des droits de l'homme. Textes préfacés et annotés* (Paris: Flammarion, 1989).

28 E.g., Diderot in Benot, *Diderot*, 187.

29 Seymour Drescher, *Econocide, British Slavery in the Era of Abolition* (Pittsburgh: Pittsburgh University Press, 1977).

30 Duchet, *Anthropologie et histoire*, 177; Michèle Duchet, *Le Partage des savoirs* (Paris: La Découverte, 1985).

31 *Archives Parlementaires* 25, 740. To be fair, the same Grégoire was accused more than once of inciting black rebellion, but the specific evidence was quite weak. See for instance, *Archives Parlementaires*, vol. 10 (session of 28 November 1789), 383. See also Carl Ludwig Lokke, *France and the Colonial Question: A Study of French Contemporary Opinion* (New York: Columbia University Press, 1932), 125–135; Sala-Molins, *Misères des Lumières*, passim.

32 M. Schwartz (Marie Jean-Antoine Nicolas Caritat, Marquis de Condorcet), *Réflexions sur l'esclavage des Nègres* (Neufchatel et Paris, 1781).

33 Lokke, *France and the Colonial Question*, 115.

34 Actually, the two remarkable exceptions I am willing to concede are Jean-Pierre Marat and Félicité Sonthonax.

35 To be sure, there were oral and written texts of which the philosophical import became increasingly explicit as the Revolution advanced, from the speeches reportedly given at the gatherings that preceded the insurrection to the Haitian Constitution of 1805. But these are primarily political texts marking immediate goals or recent victories. Up to the first post-independence writings of Boisrond-Tonnere, there were no full-time intellectuals to engage in speech acts one step removed from the political battles, as in the French and the American revolutions, the later anticolonial struggles of Latin America, Asia, or Africa, or the revolutions that claimed a Marxist ancestry.

36 Clearly, many *gens de couleur* and especially mulatto plantation owners had internalized white racial prejudice. Further, some had quite objective reasons to argue for the maintenance of slavery. European debates, and especially the French Revolution, provided them a platform to argue for their interest and to voice their prejudices. See Julien Raimond, *Observations sur l'origine et les progrès du préjugé des colons blancs contre les hommes de couleur; sur les inconvéniens de le perpétuer; la nécessité de le détruire* (Paris: Belin, 1791); Michel-Rolph Trouillot, "Motion in the System: Coffee, Color and Slavery in Eighteenth-Century Saint-Domingue," *Review* 5, no. 3 (A Journal of the Fernand Braudel Center for the Study of Economies, Historical Systems and Civilizations): 331–388; Michel-Rolph Trouillot, "The Inconvenience of Freedom: Free People of Color and the Political Aftermath of Slavery in Dominica and Saint-Domingue/Haiti," in *The Meaning of Freedom: Economics, Politics and Culture after Slavery*, ed. F. McGlynn and S. Drescher (Pittsburgh: University of Pittsburgh Press, 1992), 147–182; Geggus, "Racial Equality," 1290–1308. On the rejection of racial prejudice by mulatto leader André Rigaud, see Ernst Trouillot, *Prospections d'Histoire. Choses de Saint-Domingue et d'Haïti* (Port-au-Prince: Imprimerie de l'Etat, 1961), 25–36.

37 *Archives Parlementaires*, vol. 34 (session of 30 October 1791), 521; see also 437–38; 455–58; 470, 522–531.

38 Robin Blackburn, *The Overthrow of Colonial Slavery* (London and New York: Verso, 1988), 133.

39 Baillio, *L'Anti-Brissot, par un petit blanc de Saint-Domingue* (Paris: Chez Girardin, Club Littéraire et Politique, 1791); Baillio, *Un Mot de vérité sur les malheurs de Saint-Domingue* (Paris, 1791); Milscent, *Sur les troubles de Saint-Domingue* (Paris: Imp. du Patriote français, 1791); Anonymous, *Adresse au roi et pièces relatives à la députation des citoyens de Nantes, à l'occasion de la révolte des Noirs à*

Saint-Domingue. Arrêté de la Municipalité de Nantes (Le Cap, n.d. [1792?]); Anonymous, *Pétition des citoyens commerçants, colons, agriculteurs, manufacturiers et autres de la ville de Nantes; Lettre des commissaires de la Société d'agriculture, des arts et du commerce de la dite ville aux commissaires, de l'assemblée coloniale de la partie française de Saint-Domingue, et réponse des commissaires de Saint-Domingue* (Paris: Imp. de L. Potier de Lille, n.d.[1792?]).

See also the reports of the legislative committees led respectively by Charles Tarbé and Garran-Coulon: *Pieces imprimées par ordre de l'Assemblée Nationale. Colonies* (Paris: Imprimerie Nationale, 1792) and J. Ph. Garran, *Rapport sur les troubles de Saint-Domingue, fait au nom de la Commission des Colonies, des Comités de Salut Public, de Législation et de Marine, réunis* (Paris: Imprimerie Nationale, 1787–89). Further references to these debates are in the *Archives Parlementaires*, notably vol. 35, (sessions of 1 December 1791, 3 December 1791, 9 December 1791, 10 December 1791), 475–492; 535–546; 672–675; 701–710. Blangilly's speech was read on 10 December 1791. *Archives Parlementaires*, vol. 35, 713–716.

40 Cited by Cauna, *Au temps des isles à sucre*, 223. Emphasis added.

41 Blanchelande, *Précis de Blanchelande sur son accusation* (Paris: Imprimerie de N.-H. Nyon, 1793); Anonymous, *Extrait d'une lettre sur les malheurs de SAINT-DOMINGUE en général, et pricipalement sur l'incendie de la ville du CAP FRANÇAIS* (Paris: Au jardin égalité pavillon, 1794?); Anonymous, *Conspirations, trahisons et calomnies dévoilées et dénoncées par plus de dix milles français réfugiés au Continent de l'Amérique*, (Paris?: 1793); [Mme. Lavaux], *Réponse aux calomnies coloniales de Saint-Domingue. L'épouse du républicain Lavaux, gouverneur général (par intérim) des îles françaises sous le vent, à ses concitoyens* (Paris: Imp. de Pain, n.d.); J. Raimond et al., *Preuves complettes* [sic] *et matérielles du projet des colons pour mener les colonies à l'indépendance, tirées de leurs propres écrits* (Paris: De l'imprimerie de l'Union, n.d. [1792?]).

42 *Cobbet's Political Register*, vol. 1. (1802), 286.

43 Benot, *La Démence.*

44 Historically, of course, the respective denials of the Haitian Revolution, of the relevance of slavery, and of the Holocaust have quite different ideological motivations, social acceptance, and political impact.

45 See chap. 2. See also David Nicholls, *From Dessalines to Duvalier: Race, Colour and National Independence in Haiti* (London: Macmillian Caribbean, 1988); and Michel-Rolph Trouillot, *Haiti: State against Nation. The Origins and Legacy of Duvalierism.* (New York and London: Monthly Review Press, 1990).

46 The Haitian Revolution sparked the interests of abolitionists in the United States and especially in England, where there were a few calls for support. But even British abolitionists showed much ambivalence toward the Haitian people and their forcibly acquired independence. Blackburn, *The Overthrow of Colonial Slavery*, 252–52; Greggus, "Racial Equality."

47 Trouillot, *Haiti: State against Nation.*

48 One of the rare studies of the Polish legions in Saint-Domingue is Jan Pachonski and Reuel Wilson, *Poland's Caribbean Tragedy. A Study of Polish Legions in the Haitian War of Independence, 1802–1803* (Boulder: East European Monographs, 1986), unfortunately marred by a number of mistakes.

Hobsbawn mentions the Haitian Revolution once in the notes, twice in the text: the first time to say, in passing, that Toussaint Louverture was the first independent revolutionary leader of the Americas—as if that was not important; the second time (in parentheses) to note that the French Revolution "inspired" colonial uprisings. See Eric J. Hobsbawm, *The Age of Revolutions, 1789–1848* (New York: New American Library, 1962), 93, 115. If we accept that Hobsbawm is at the extreme left of Western academic historiography and a historian otherwise conscious of both the invention of tradition and the need to write a history from below, the parallel with Diderot-Raynal is amazing.

49 Blackburn, *The Overthrow of Colonial Slavery*, 251, 263.

50 Philip D. Curtin, *The Atlantic Slave Trade: A Census* (Madison: University of Wisconsin, 1969), 210–220, 34.

51 Jean Tarrade, "Le Commerce colonial de la France à la fin de l'ancien régime: l'évolution du système de l'exclusif de 1763 à 1789," 2 vols. (Thèse pour le doctorat d'état, Paris: Université de Paris, Faculté des Lettres et des Sciences Humaines, [1969]1972). Robert Stein, *The French Sugar Business* (Baton Rouge: Lousiana State University Press, 1988).

52 One circular of the pro-slavery forces argues forcibly along such lines: "The Société des Amis des Noirs wishes to bring into question in the National Assembly the abandonment of our colonies, the abolition of the slave trade and the liberty of our Negroes. If only one of these points is decreed, there would no longer exist commerce or manufacture in France," in Daniel P. Resnick, "The Société des Amis des Noirs and the Abolition of Slavery," *French Historical Studies*, vol. 7 (1972), 558–569, 564. See also *Archives Parlementaires*, vol. 10 (session of 26 November 1789), 263–65; vol. 35 (session of 6 December 1791), 607–608.

53 Resnick, "The Société des Amis des Noirs," 561. There is now a growing literature on public debates on slavery, race, and colonialism in revolutionary

France, with quite a few titles in English. See Robin Blackburn, "Anti-Slavery and the French Revolution," *History Today* 41 (November 1991): 19–25; Boulle, "In Defense of Slavery"; Serge Daget, "A Model of the French Abolitionist Movement," in *Anti-Slavery, Religion and Reform*, eds. Christine Bolt and Seymour Drescher (Folkstone, England: W. Dawson, and Hamden, Connecticut: Archon Books, 1980); Seymour Drescher, "Two Variants of Anti-Slavery: Religious Organization and Social Mobilization in Britain and France, 1780–1870," in *Anti-Slavery, Religion and Reform*, 43–63; Seymour Drescher, "British Way, French Way: Opinion Building and Revolution in the Second French Emancipation," *American Historical Review* 96, no. 3 (1991): 709–734; Geggus, "Racial Equality," 1290–1308; Jean Tarrade, "Les Colonies et les Principes de 1789: Les Assemblées Révolutionnaires face au problème de l'esclavage," *Revue française d'histoire d'outre-mer* 76 (1979): 9–34.

Many relevant passages are also in Cohen, *The French Encounter with Africans*, and Blackburn, *The Overthrow of Colonial Slavery*, especially chaps. 5 and 6. The most comprehensive book on the subject is Benot, *Le Révolution française*.

54 An increasing number of historians are also exposing the silence. Geggus, "Racial Equality," 1290–1291; Benot, *La Révolution française*, 205–216; Tarrade, "Les colonies et les principes de 1789," 9–34.

55 Jacques Marseille and Nadeije Laneyrie-Dagen (eds.), *Les Grands évènements de l'histoire du monde*, La Mémoire de l'humanité (Paris: Larousse, 1992).

56 French historians could not claim to have missed these two books: Césaire was at the time one of the most prominent blacks writing in French. James was published by the prestigious Parisian house of Gallimard. Aimé Césaire, *Toussaint Louverture. La Révolution française et le problème colonial* (Paris: Présence africaine, 1962). P. I. R. [*sic*] James, *Les Jacobins noirs* (Paris: Gallimard, 1949).

57 These collective works include notably, François Furet and Mona Ouzouf, *Dictionnaire critique de la Révolution française* (Paris: Flammarion, 1988); Jean Tulard, Jean-François Fayard et Alfred Fierro, *Histoire et dictionnaire de la Révolution (1789–1799)* (Paris: Robert Laffont, 1987); Michel Vovelle, ed., *L'Etat de la France pendant la Révolution* (Paris: La Découverte, 1988). In such arid land, this last compilation has the merit to attribute a few pages to colonial issues, written by U.S. historican Robert Forster and the indefatigable Yves Benot. On the celebrations, see Sala-Molins, *Les Misères des Lumières*.

58 E.g., Yvan Debbash, "Le Marronage: Essai sur la désertion de l'esclave antillais," *L'Année sociologique* (1961): 1–112; (1962): 117–195.

59 One example among others. David Geggus and Jean Fouchard agree in suggesting that a royalist conspiracy could have provoked the revolt of 1791. But

Fouchard notes this possibility in a book that remains one of the epic monuments of Haitian history. Geggus, in turn, concludes that if royalist participation is proved, "the autonomy of the slave insurrection will find itself considerably diminished." Robin Blackburn, who notes this disparity between the two authors, rightly finds Geggus's conclusion "curious" (Blackburn, *The Overthrow of Colonial Slavery*, 210). See Jean Fouchard, *The Haitian Maroons: Liberty or Death* (New York: Blyden Press, 1981; original printing, 1972).

60 See Julius S. Scott III, "The Common Wind: Currents of Afro-American Communications in the Era of the Haitian Revolution" (Ph.D. diss., Duke University, 1986).

61 See Robert Stein, *Léger Félicité Sonthonax: The Lost Sentinel of the Republic* (Rutherford: Fairleigh Dickinson, 1985); Benot, *La Révolution.*

62 Stein, *Léger Félicité Sonthonax*; Cauna, *Au temps des isles*; David Geggus, *Slavery, War and Revolution: The British Occupation of St. Domingue, 1793–1798* (Oxford, New York: Oxford University Press, 1982). The "revolution" in Geggus's title is the *French* revolution. He has since extended his use of the word to include Haitian achievements.

63 Eugene Genovese, *From Rebellion to Revolution* (New York: Vintage, 1981 [1979]). Blackburn, *The Overthrow of Colonial Slavery.*

64 Thomas Madiou, *Histoire d'Haïti*, 7 vols. (Port-au-Prince: Henri Deschamps, 1987–89 [1847–1904]); A. Beaubrun Ardouin, *Études sur l'histoire d'Haïti* (Port-au-Prince: François Dalencourt, 1958). See Catts Pressoir, Ernst Trouillot, and Hénock Trouillot, *Historiographie d'Haïti* (Mexico: Instituto Panamericano de Geografía e Historia, 1953); Michel-Rolph Trouillot, *Ti difé boulé sou istoua Ayiti* (New York: Koléskion Lakansièl, 1977); Michel-Rolph Trouillot, *Haiti: State against Nation.*

65 See Carolyn Fick, *The Making of Haïti: The Saint-Domingue Revolution from Below* (Knoxville: University of Tennessee Press, 1990); Claude B. Auguste and Marcel B. Auguste, *L'Expédition Leclerc, 1801–1803* (Port-au-Prince: Imprimerie Henri Deschamps, 1985). Fick remains much too close to the epic rhetoric of the Haitian tradition. Her treatment of resistance is overly ideological and skews her reading of the evidence in the direction of heroism. Nevertheless, her book adds more to the empirical bank on Saint-Domingue than most recent works in the epic tradition. David Geggus's ongoing research remains empirically impeccable. One wishes that it would continue to move further away from the discourse of banalization and would spell out explicitly, one day, some of its hidden assumptions. The work by the Auguste brothers on the French expedition comes closer to finding a tone that treats its material with ideological respect without falling into a celebration or extrapolating from the evidence. It is well grounded into archival research, yet it does not make concessions to the banalizing discourse.

66 Fernand Braudel, *Civilization and Capitalism*, 3 vols. (New York: Harper & Row, 1981–1992); Eric R. Wolf, *Europe and the People without History* (Berkeley: University of California Press, 1982); Marc Ferro, *Histoire des colonisations. Des conquêtes aux indépendances, XIIIe–XXe siècles* (Paris: Seuil, 1994).

4 Good Day, Columbus

1 Rachel Arié, *L'Espagne musulmane au temps des Nasrides (1232–1492)* (Paris: Éditions E. de Brocard, 1973); Charles Julian Bishko, "The Spanish and Portuguese Reconquest, 1095–1492," in *Studies in Medieval Spanish Frontier History* (London: Variorum Reprints, 1980; reprinted from Setton and Hazard, eds., *A History of the Crusades* (Madison: University of Wisconsin Press, [1975], 1980 396–456).

2 The influence of nearly eight centuries of Islamic control over one or another of the dominions of Europe is undeniable. See S. M. Imamuddin, *Muslim Spain, 711–1492 A.D.*, Medieval Iberian Texts and Studies (Leiden: E. J. Brill, 1981); Robert I. Burns, *Muslims, Chrisitians and Jews in the Crusader Kingdom of Valencia* (Cambridge: Cambridge University Press, 1984); Allan Harris Cutler and Helen Elmquist Cutler, *The Jew as Ally of the Muslim. Medieval Roots of Anti-Semitism* (Notre Dame: University of Notre Dame Press, 1986); Claudio Sanchez-Albornoz, *L'Espagne musulmane*, trans. Claude Farragi (Paris: OPU/Publisud., 1985 [1946–1973]). Also, whereas the Christian victors expelled the Jews, the capitulation treaties protected Islamic cultural practices, including religion. See Arié, *L'Espagne musulmane*; Irving, "Reconquest of Granada"; Bishko, "The Spanish and Portuguese Reconquest"; Burns's book, *Muslims, Christians and Jews*, summarizes nicely the different approaches to the study of Muslim-Christian contact.

3 J. M. Wallace-Hadrill, *The Barbarian West, 400–1000* (Oxford and New York: Basil Blackwell, [1965] 1988); Bishko. "The Spanish and Portuguese Reconquest"; Cutler and Cutler, *The Jew as Ally of the Muslim.*

4 Bishko, "The Spanish and Portuguese Reconquest."

5 Isabella had summoned Columbus to Santa Fe, the town she had built near Granada, during the siege, to serve as military headquarters and as a symbol of Chrisitian determination. Antonio Rumeu de Amas, *Nueva Luz sobre las Capitulaciones de Santa Fe de 1492 Concertadas entre les Reyes Católicos y Cristóbal Colón.*

Estudio Institucional y Diplomático (Madrid: Consejo Superior de Investigaciones Científicas, 1985), contends that serious negotiations between royal secretary Juan de Colomba and Fr. Juan Pérez, Columbus's sponsor, started on January 2, 1492, the very day the Christian flag was raised over the Alhambra. The final mandate was drawn up in April 1492.

6 Biographers agree that the decade Columbus spent in Portugal was the formative period of his life. Unfortunately, little documentation is available on that period. See Samuel Eliot Morison, *Christopher Columbus, Mariner* (New York: New American Library, 1983), 12–16; Gianni Granzotto, *Christopher Columbus* (Garden City: Doubleday, 1985), 34–47; William D. Phillips, Jr., and Carla Rahn Phillips, *The Worlds of Christopher Columbus* (Cambridge: Cambridge University Press, 1992), 94–97.

7 Thomas Gomez, *L'Invention de l'Amérique. Rêve et réalités de la conquête* (Paris: Abier, 1993), 188–200.

8 Roy Preiswerk and Dominique Perrot, *Ethnocentrism and History. Africa, Asia and Indian America in Western Textbooks* (New York, London, Lagos: Nok Publishers, 1978), 105.

9 Camacho Juan Rafael Quesada and Magda Zavala, eds., *500 años: Holocausto o Descubrimiento?* (San Jose: Editorial Universitaria Centroamericana, 1991). Justin Thorens et al., eds., *1492. Le Choc des deux mondes* (Geneva: UNESCO/La Différence, 1993).

10 Vitorino Magalhaes Godinho, "Rôle du Portugal aux XVe–XVIe siècles. Qu'est-ce que découvrir veut dire? Les nouveaux mondes et un monde nouveau," in J. Thorens et al., *1492. Le Choc*, 57.

11 On naming and power, see Michel-Rolph Trouillot, *Peasants and Capital. Dominica in the World Economy*, Johns Hopkins Studies in Atlantic History and Culture (Baltimore and London: The Johns Hopkins University Press, 1988), 27; "Discourses of Rule and the Acknowledgement of the Peasantry in Dominica, W.I., 1838–1928," *American Ethnologist* 16 (4) (1989), 704–718. See also chap. 2, above.

12 To bring the point home to a U.S. audience, I will draw on a local analogy. In spite of its legal murkiness and its terminological awkwardness, the notion of "date rape" is both a conceptual and a political victory for actual rape victims. It desanitizes some facts of rape and makes possible narratives that were previously forbidden *as narratives of rape*. Facts that were thought to be clear can at least be presented for judgment to a court of law. Semantic ambiguities aside, for victims of rape, this is not at all a trivial matter.

13 On that score, the Quadricentennial celebrations of the landfall provide the clearest example of public history on a global stage. For different reasons, in the early 1890s both Spain and the United States enlisted the smooth participation of a number of states on both sides of the Atlantic. They were not successful in 1992.

14 Centennials themselves are elaborate variations on the annual theme. They are most often fashioned around an event that has been celebrated yearly at a fixed date—even if by a few. They may, in turn, revitalize an annual cycle, as we will see later.

15 These three ensembles are dealt with unequally here, and I do not claim to exhaust all modes of appropriation of Columbus and his landfall within each of them. Latin America in particular, where constructions about Columbus are complex and numerous, is shortchanged in the discussion that follows. See Edmundo O'Gorman, *The Invention of America: An Inquiry into the Historical Nature of the New World and the Meaning of its History* (Bloomington: Indiana University Press, 1961); John Leddy Phelan, *The Millenial Kingdom of the Franciscans in the New World* (Berkeley: University of California Press, 1970). But my point is not to show what images of Columbus look like in each of these three ensembles or even to construct an equilateral triangle with sketches from the three. Rather, this is a narrative about narratives of power that aims at no center itself—except, of course, the nondescript place that Columbus stumbled upon in the middle of this nowhere they now call the Carribbean.

16 Michel-Rolph Trouillot, "Anthropology and the Savage Slot: The Poetics and Politics of Otherness," in *Recapturing Anthropology: Working in the Present*, ed. Richard G. Fox, (Santa Fe: School of American Research Press, 1991), 17–44.

17 Lewis Hanke, *Aristotle and the American Indians* (London: Hollis and Carter, 1959), 2–3; 124. Gomez, *L'Invention de l'Amérique*, 281.

18 Until the 1830s, for instance, there may have been three times more literary or musical works about an American figure like Montezuma (including that by Vivaldi) than about Columbus.

19 Reflecting on the invention of traditions in the United States, Eric Hobsbawm rightly insists that "Americans had to be made" in ways Europeans did not need to be. See Eric Hobsbawm, "Mass-Producing Traditions: Europe, 1870–1914," in *The Invention of Tradition*, ed. E. Hobsbawm and T. Ranger. (Cambridge: Cambridge University Press, 1983), 279. This production of traditions started in the United States much earlier than Hobsbawm seems to think and perhaps earlier than in Europe since North America was perceived as having no authentic traditions.

20 On the Tammany Society, see Edwin Patrick Kilroe, *Saint Tammany and the Origin of the Society of Tammany or Columbian Order in the City of New York* (New York: Columbia University Press, 1913); and Jerome Mushkat, *Tammany: The Evolution of a Political Machine, 1789–1865* (Syracuse: Syracuse University Press, 1971). Columbus's landfall was also celebrated in Baltimore and Boston in 1792. See Herbert B. Adams, "Columbus and His Discovery of America," in *Columbus and His Discovery of America*, eds. H. B. Adams and H. Wood, Johns Hopkins University Studies in Historical and Political Science, 10th series (Baltimore: The Johns Hopkins University Press, 1892), 7–39; Reid Badger, *The Great American Fair: The World's Columbia Exposition and American Culture* (Chicago: N. Hall, 1979). The first permanent monument to Columbus in the United States may have been that erected by the Chevalier d'Anmour, the French consul to Baltimore (Adams, "Columbus and His Discovery of America," 30–31). Still, New York tends to be the most popular reference for early Columbian celebrations, proving that even traditions about traditions are created unequal. On early monuments to Columbus in the United States, see Charles Weathers Bump, "Public Memorials to Columbus," in Adams and Wood, *Columbus and His Discovery of America*, 69–88.

21 Columbus died in Spain in 1505. More than thirty years later, his remains were transferred to Santo Domingo, then supposedly to Havana and/or Seville. Where they are now remains a matter of controversy, in spite of Santo Domingo's edge among the favorite locations.

22 The acknowledgement that the rules for classification had changed was quite candid on the part of the early colonists. It declined somewhat in the eighteenth and nineteenth centuries to reappear with political and cultural nationalisms of various kinds in the twentieth century. See Anthony Pagden, "Identity Formation in Spanish America," in *Colonial Identity in the Atlantic World*, eds. N. Canny and A. Pagden (Princeton: Princeton University Press, 1987), 51–93; Stuart Schwartz, "The Formation of a Colonial Identity in Brazil," in *Colonial Identity in the Atlantic World*, 15–50; Magnus Mörner, *Race Mixture in the History of Latin America* (Boston: Little, Brown, 1967); Magnus Mörner, ed., *Race and Class in Latin America* (New York: Columbia University Press, 1970).

23 Mörner, *Race Mixture; Race and Class in Latin America*; Schwartz, "The Formation of a Colonial Identity in Brazil"; Pagden, "Identity Formation in Spanish America"; Marvin Harris, *Patterns of Race in the Americas* (New York: Norton Library, [1964] 1974); Nina De Friedemann, "The Fiesta of the Indian in Quibdó, Colombia," in *Ethnicity in the Americas*, ed. F. Henry (The Hague and Paris: Mouton, 1976), 291–300.

This does not suggest that Latin America stands outside the international hierarchy of races, religions, and cultures, or that native Americans in that region do not encounter prejudice. Rather both discourses and institutionalized practices of discrimination allow much more flexibility to the actors than, say, the rigid U.S. system–to the point where phenotype alone does not determine the socio-racial denomination of specific individuals. In fact, at times, the reverse can be true: individuals of known "Indian" ancestry can become "white." See Eric R. Wolf, *Sons of the Shaking Earth* (Chicago and London: University of Chicago Press, 1959), 236. The treatment of black populations and the ways that boundaries defining blackness and whiteness are erected is also relevant to this argument. Marvin Harris, who rightly criticizes naive claims of Latin American racial harmony, admits that "it is definitely verifiable that all hybrids were not and are not forced back into a sharply separated Negro group by application of a rule of descent. This was true during slavery and it was true after slavery. . . ." See Harris, *Patterns of Race*. This was even truer of the native Americans.

24 Schwartz, "The Formation of a Colonial Identity in Brazil," 30. See also Pagden, "Identity Formation in Spanish America."

25 Cited by Mörner, *Race Mixture*, 86.

26 Mörner, *Race Mixture*; Manning Nash, "The Impact of Mid-Nineteenth Economic Change Upon the Indians of Middle America," in Mörner, ed., *Race and Class in Latin America*, 181–83.

27 These ideological traits of the discourse on culture and ethnicity in Latin America are so strong that they spill over into academic literature. Many scholars speak of Latin American groups as if they were peculiar biological blends—café au lait type mixtures—of otherwise "pure" pre-Conquest entities: Indian, African, Spanish, Portuguese (e.g., Mörner, *Race Mixture* and *Race and Class*). Similarly, "the Indian Legacy" of Spanish America is often assumed, rather than demonstrated, by "native" cultural historians in particular (e.g., Mariano Picón-Salas, *A Cultural History of Spanish America from Conquest to Independence* (Berkeley: University of California Press, 1967).

28 Lydio F. Tomasi, ed., *Italian Americans. New Perspectives in Italian Immigration and Ethnicity* (New York: Center for Migration Studies of New York, 1985); Charles Speroni, "The Development of the Columbus Day Pageant of San Francisco," reproduced in *The Folklore of American Holidays*, ed. H. Cohen and T. P. Coffin (Detroit: Gale Research, 1987), 301–02).

There are vague mentions of Columbus Day celebrations by Italian-Americans as early as the 1840s, especially after the creation of the Colombo Guard by Genoese immigrants in New York. See Lydio F. Tomasi, ed., *The Italian in America: The Progressive View, 1891–1914* (New York: Center for Migration Studies, 1972), 79.

29 Christopher Kauffmann, *Faith and Fraternalism. The History of the Knights of Columbus, 1882–1982* (New York: Harper & Row, 1982).

30 Kaufmann, *Faith and Fraternalism*, 79–81.

31 Bessie Louise Pierce, *Public Opinion and the Teaching of History in the United States* (New York: Alfred A. Knopf, 1926).

32 Hobsbawn, "Mass-Producing Traditions"; Eric Hobsbawn, *The Age of Empire, 1875–1914* (New York: Pantheon, 1987); Salvador Bernabeu Albert, *1892: El IV Centenario del descubrimiento de America en España: Coyonjuta y Commemoraciones* (Madrid: Ceonsejo Superior de Investigaciones Cientificas, 1987); Timothy Mitchell, *Colonizing Egypt* (Cambridge: Cambridge University Press, 1988); Reid Badger, *The Great America Fair: The World's Columbia Exposition and American Culture* (Chicago: N. Hall, 1979).

33 Raymond Carr, *Spain, 1808–1939*, Oxford History of Modern Europe (Oxford: Clarendon Press, 1966); Melchor Fernandez Almagro, *Cánovas. Su vida y su política* (Madrid: Ediciones Tebas, Collección Políticos y Financieros, 1972); Hobsbawm, *The Age of Empire*.

34 Albert, *1892*, 19.

35 My account of the quadricentennial activities is drawn primarily from Albert, *1892*. On Spain at the time, see Carr, *Spain, 1808–1939*; on Cánovas, see Almagro, *Cánovas*.

36 They were France, the United Kingdom, Italy, Belgium, Russia, Austria, Holland, Denmark, Germany, Portugal, Mexico, Argentina, the Dominican Republic, El Salvador, Guatemala, Costa Rica, Columbia, Uruguay, Bolivia, Peru, Chile, Brazil, Haiti, and the United States.

37 Albert, *El IV Centenario*; Louis de Vorsey, Jr. and J. Parker, eds., *The Columbus Landfall Problem: Islands and Controversy* (Detroit: Wayne State University Press, 1982).

38 Topics in Madrid and elsewhere varied from "Marriage and Divorce in Private International Law," to the possibility of a military alliance tying Spain and Portugal to Latin America, to the relevance of philosophical positivism for the writing of history.

39 Cited by Albert, *El IV Centenario*, 123.

40 Cited by Badger, *The Great America Fair*, 120.

41 Badger, *The Great America Fair*, 132. On the Chicago Exposition, see John Joseph Flinn, ed., *Official Guide to the World's Columbian Exposition*, handbook ed. (Chicago: Columbian Guide, 1893); Rand McNally and Co., *Handbook of the World's Columbian Exposition* (Chicago: Rand McNally, 1893); Badger, *The Great America Fair* and Robert W. Rydell, *All the World Is a Fair. Visions of Empire at American International Expositions, 1876–1916* (Chicago: University of Chicago Press, 1984).

42 Years before, the United States had boycotted a similar project by Bolívar. Blaine himself did not witness the opening of the fair. He died in January 1893, months after submitting his resignation to President Harrison.

43 Albert T. Volwiller, ed., *The Correspondence Between Benjamin Harrison and James G. Blaine, 1882–1893*, Memoirs of the American Philosophical Society, vol. 14 (Philadelphia: American Philosophical Society, 1940); Leslie Manigat, *L'Amérique latine au XXe siècle 1889–1929*, L'Univers Contemporain, ed. Jean Baptiste Duroselle (Paris: L'Université de Paris, Institut d'Histoire de Relations Internationales, 1973); Lester D. Langley, *America and the Americas: The United States in the Western Hemisphere* (Athens: University of Georgia Press, 1989); Homer E. Socolofsky and Allan B. Spetter, *The Presidency of Benjamin Harrison*, American Presidency Series (Lawrence: University of Kansas, 1987); David Healy, *Drive to Hegemony. The United States in the Caribbean, 1898–1917* (Madison: University of Wisconsin Press, 1988).

44 Flinn, *Official Guide to the World's Columbian Exposition*, 7–8.

45 I. W. Howerth, "Are the Italians a Dangerous Class?" *The Charities Review—A Journal of Practical Sociology* IV (1894): 17–40.

46 Tomasi, *The Italian in America*; Badger, *The Great America Fair*, 85.

47 "An Act Fixing and Establishing the Permanent and Temporary Seats of Government," *Journal of the House of Representatives of the State of Ohio* (Chillecothe: J. S. Collins, 1812). "An Act to Amend an Act Fixing," *Journal of the House of Representatives of the State of Ohio* (Zanesville: Dadid Cham, 1816). John Kilbourn, *The Ohio Gazetteer or Topographical Dictionary*, 2d ed. (Columbus: Smith and Griswold, 1816), 3 and passim; 3d ed., (Albany, New York: Loomis, 1817); 5th ed., (Columbus, Ohio: Griswold, 1818); 6th ed., (Columbus, Ohio: Bailhache & Scott, 1819). Caleb Atwater, *A History of the State of Ohio, Natural and Civil*, 2d ed. (Cincinnati: Glenzen & Shepard, 1838). James Silk Buckingham, *The Eastern and Western United States of America*, vol. 2 (London: Fisher, Son, 1842). James H. Perkins, *Annals of the West* (Cincinnati: James R. Albach, 1847). Henry Howe, *Historical Collections of Ohio* (Cincinnati: Bradley and Anthony, 1848). W. H. Carpenter and T. S. Arthur, eds., *The History of Ohio, from its Earli-*

est Settlement to the Present Time (Philadelphia: Lippincott, Grambo, 1854). Jacob Henry Studer, *Columbus, Ohio: Its History, Resources and Progress* (Columbus: J. H. Studer, 1873).

To be sure, all these documents could have missed the trace of a connection between the Genoese navigator and the Ohio town. My point is that even if such a trace existed then, it had little significance in and out of Columbus, Ohio. Both Buckingham and Howe had an interest in the origins of town names. Neither mentions the Genoese.

48 Bump, "Public Memorials to Columbus," 70.

49 *Official Guidebook, AmeriFlora '92: April 20–October 12* (Columbus: Marbro Guide Publications, 1992). There are many references to "the largest city in the world named after the great explorer" in recent mentions of the connections, echoes of Chicago 1893 and the U.S. appetite for size.

50 Sidney W. Mintz, "Goodbye, Columbus: Second Thoughts on the Caribbean Region at Mid-Millennium," Walter Rodney Memorial Lecture, May 1993 (Coventry: University of Warwick, 1994).

51 Hence, the limited relevance of the terminological debate about "blacks" versus "Negroes," "Afro-," or "African-Americans." The central problem here is not how to designate U.S. citizens of known African descent but how to reconcile their blackness with the second half of the compound. Whether or not some Asian-Americans or Hispanic-Americans will become honorary whites, as have all Irish and Italian immigrants before them, and whether this new inclusion will burst open the second half of these compounds is an open question.

52 Tomasi, *The Italian in America*, 78.

53 Columbus Day did not become a federal holiday in the United States until 1968.

54 This "American" Columbus was modified somewhat in old world territories taken by the United States. Further decontextualized, October 12 became Discovery Day in Hawaii and Guam, places where Columbus never set foot alive, but where chunks of the myth followed U.S. power.

55 October 12 is a fixed holiday in at least twelve former colonies of Spain, under different labels, including "Day of the Americas" in addition to those cited above. There are numerous variations on the theme. Panama, whose Latin legitimacy has sometimes been questioned because of its United States-sponsored birth, celebrates Latin American Nations Days on October 12. In Cuba, discovery-oriented celebrations were toned down by the revolutionary government which, in turn, promoted the celebration of the launching of the war of independence on October 10. Peru does not set Columbus Day as a fixed holiday but celebrates National Dignity Day on October 9. The situation is quite different in countries where the influence of Spain is less obvious. Except for the United States and Canada, none of the American countries that bear more strongly the imprint of one of Spain's former colonial competitors celebrates October 12. For instance, Trinidad celebrates the first European landfall on its shores on August 4. Haiti celebrates its own "discovery" on December 5.

56 There are many twists to the manipulation of history and of current calendars in the construction of ethnicity. In Caño Mochuelo, Columbia, October 12 is "The Day of the Indian," the occasion for one of the many regional fiestas which, according to De Friedemann, perpetuate Indian stereotypes and act as a "cultural mechanism of subordination." Friedemann, "The Fiesta of the Indian in Quibdó, Colombia," 293.

57 Christopher Columbus, *The Diario of Christopher Columbus's First Voyage to America, 1492–1493* (Norman: University of Oklahoma Press, 1989), 63.

58 Columbus, *The Diario*; Columbus, *The Voyage of Christopher Columbus*, ed. John Cummins (London: Weindenfeld and Nicholson, 1992), 93.

5 The Presence in the Past

1 William Styron, "Slavery's Pain, Disney's Gain," *The New York Times*, 4 August 1994.

2 Jorge Luis Borges, "Pierre Ménard, Author of Don Quixote," in *The Overwrought Urn*, ed. C. Kaplan, (New York: Pegasus, 1969 [original Spanish 1938]). On Ménard's novel as performance, see A. J. Cascardi, "Remembering," *Review of Metaphysics 38* (1984): 275–302.

3 Many historians and Civil War buffs had fought the project because they felt that the proposed park would blot out important war sites. Environmentalists, in turn, had raised an uproar about crowding and traffic congestion. In both cases, the loudest objections focused more on the proposed site than on the intrinsic value of the project. In the same tone, Disney's official announcement was that the company would look for a "less controversial" site. Some analysts saw in the announcement a graceful way for Disney to abandon the project altogether. *The Wall Street Journal* (29 September 1994), 3; *The New York Times* (29 September 1994); (30 September 1994).

4 I am not assuming that either Ménard, or Borges himself espouses or expresses a coherent philosophy of history. I am not even assuming that Borges's main theme here is history. Obviously, I am using the parody within my own frame. I am satisfied, however, that this use is justifiable. For extended treatments of "Pierre Ménard," see Raphaël Latouche, *Borges ou l'hypothèse de l'auteur* (Paris: Balland, 1989), especially pt. III, "L'oeuvre invisible. Pierre Ménard auteur du Quichotte," 170–210. Emilio Carilla, *Jorge Luis Borges autor de 'Pierre Ménard' (y otros estudios borgesianos)*, pt. 1 (Bogota: Instituto Caro y Cuervo, 1989), 20–92. For a related theoretical use of Ménard's *Quixote*, see Cascardi, "Remembering," 291–293. For Ménard and the history of texts, see Jean-Marie Schaeffer, *Qu'est-ce qu'un genre littéraire?* (Paris: du Seuil, 1989), 131–154.

5 For a similar conclusion on the text as literary product drawing from a reading of Borges, see Schaeffer, *Qu'est-ce qu'un genre littéraire?*

6 Borges, "Pierre Ménard," 23.

7 Cascardi, "Remembering," 289.

8 Pierre Vidal-Naquet, *Les Assassins de la mémoire: "un Eichmann de papier" et autres essais sur le révisionnisme* (Paris: La Découverte, 1987); Pierre Weill, "L'anniversaire impossible," *Le Nouvel Observateur* 1579, 9–15 February 1995, 51. The divergences between Vidal-Naquet's stance and mine are mostly—but not only—terminological. He calls "memory" a living relation to the past, in part because he believes in a scientific history based implicitly on a nineteenth-century model of science. I explicitly reject that model both for the natural sciences and for the systematic historical investigations performed by professionals. For the record, Weill's statement should not be dismissed as the individual complaint of a Jew maladjusted within France's social structure: he is the president of the powerful Sofres group.

9 Francis Fukuyama, *The End of History and the Last Man* (New York: The Free Press, 1992).

10 David McCullough, James McPherson, David Brian Davis are among the historians who addressed wide audiences on some of these controversies in public forums or in newspapers.

11 In France, leading members of the guild express themselves regularly in daily or weekly publications. François Furet or Emmanuel Leroy Ladurie are not penalized for writing in *Le Nouvel Observateur* or *Le Monde*. Some of the most famous names in German history fought the Historierke debate on the uniqueness of the Holocaust in the pages of daily and weekly newspapers. And the public debate itself was launched by philosopher-sociologist Jürgen Habermas.

12 Jacques Le Goff, *History and Memory* (New York: Columbia University Press, 1992).

13 In the 1970s, some professional historians, notably Jean Chesneaux and Paul Thompson, made a passionate case for academic historians to explicitly position themselves vis-à-vis their present. See Jean Chesneaux, *Du passé faisons table rase* (Paris: Maspero, 1976); Paul Thompson, *The Voice of The Past: Oral History* (Oxford, New York: Oxford University Press, 1978).

14 See Tzvetan Todorov, *Les Morales de l'histoire* (Paris: Bernard Grasset, 1991), chaps. 7 and 8, on the ethical differences between scholars and intellectuals.

Index